CW00531552

men with learning disabilities who sexually abuse

working together to develop response-ability

David Thompson and Hilary Brown
based on research funded by the Foundation for People with Learning Disabilities

Pavilion

Men with learning disabilities who sexually abuse

Working together to develop *response-ability*

David Thompson and Hilary Brown
based on research funded by the Mental Health Foundation

First published in 1998 as 'Response-ability'.

This edition published 2005.

Published by:

Pavilion Publishing (Brighton) Limited
Richmond House
Richmond Road
Brighton
East Sussex BN2 3RL
Telephone: 01273 623222
Fax: 01273 625526
Email: pavpub@pavilion.co.uk
www.pavpub.com

ISBN 1 84196 135 3

A Catalogue record for this pack is available from The British Library.

Editor: Jo Hathaway and Grace Fairley
Design and typesetting: Jigsaw Design (Worthing)
Printing: Ashford Press (Southampton)

Contents

  Activities

    Activity 1a: How good is your information?

    Activity 1b: Where do you stand?

    Activity 1c: Acceptable, unacceptable, inappropriate or abusive?

Case checklists

Preface

This manual was first printed in 1998 and was based on a research project funded by the Foundation for People with Learning Disabilities undertaken at the Tizard Centre, University of Kent. It filled an important gap by addressing the service needs of a uniquely disadvantaged group of service-users – men with learning disabilities who are at risk of sexually offending. Despite many changes in service models, including the introduction of person-centred planning, the basic principles set out in the book remain relevant. This edition has been updated to reflect changes in legislation – notably the introduction of new legislation on sexual offences and new frameworks on mental capacity and decision-making for people who may be unable to make some decisions themselves. These developments will assist those who are charged with intervening to protect these men and those to whom they pose a risk.

Since the time of writing, the authors have both moved on from the Tizard Centre. Dr David Thompson now works for Advocacy Partners and Professor Hilary Brown is based at the Centre for Applied Social and Psychological Development at Salomons, which is a faculty of Canterbury Christ Church University.

The authors would like to thank Jan Alcoe at Pavilion for supporting this reprint.

Acknowledgements

The research for this work was funded by the Mental Health Foundation (incorporating the Foundation for People with Learning Disabilities) and we should like to thank them for their support throughout this project. Liz Gale and Hazel Morgan particularly supported the work on behalf of the Foundation.

The project was administered at the Tizard Centre by Patricia Barton. Later versions of the text were managed by Julie Stock at The Open University.

This workbook has been based on, and designed around, a number of detailed case studies in a range of learning disability services. Two districts and their associated social services departments particularly collaborated in the work and we should like to thank them for their commitment, openness and input. We have called them **Innerborough** (an inner city local authority with high levels and indices of deprivation) and **Ruralville** (a relatively well-off coastal borough with integrated health and social services). Further details of the services and structures of these two areas are given in **Part Three** where an overview of service provision for this group of users is considered.

We should like to thank all those who have contributed to this process of fact finding and service development. These include:

- the men themselves, who have told their stories and allowed them to be used for the benefit of others (for a discussion of the problems of the men agreeing to have their stories told see Brown & Thompson, 1997a)

- senior practitioners and managers working on behalf of their agencies, who agreed to be involved in the project and who gave their time and expertise so generously throughout

- workers in services where the work was undertaken, for their willingness to share the very real difficulties and dilemmas which arose in the context of these abusive or unacceptable sexual behaviours

- the project's advisory committee, who contributed their support and expert consideration of the issues, and particularly Professor Glynis Murphy, Professor of Clinical Psychology at the Institute for Health Research, Lancaster University, who chaired the meetings

- ethical committees in both districts, who gave such thoughtful consideration to the proposal at outline stage and helped us to think through the complex ethical issues which arise in the wider context of working with learning disabled men who sexually offend

- workers who attended focus groups which helped us to determine which behaviours were problematic and helped us to uncover the, often hidden, gender dynamics which permeate this work and which have the potential to limit and distort appropriate interventions.

Introduction

The aims of this manual

This manual has been designed to assist workers in learning disability and related services who work with men who have unacceptable or abusive sexual behaviours. It is subtitled *Working together to develop* ***response-ability*** (and the original edition of this manual was titled *Response-Ability*) because we believe that it is the **ability to respond** and the explicit sharing of **responsibility** which are central to the issues of protection and intervention thrown up by difficult sexual behaviour.

Why does the manual focus on men?

It is clear from the literature on sexual offending that it is predominantly men who *sexually* abuse – whether they have learning disabilities or not. Studies gathering data using a range of methodologies consistently find that 95% or more of the perpetrators of sexual abuse are men and that the few women who abuse often do so alongside men they are involved with. This is not to exonerate those women who do sexually abuse or who abuse in other ways – women can also be intrusive, insensitive or inappropriate but they do not usually engage directly in sexual activities against the wishes of other people (Brown & Thompson, 1997c; Brown, Stein & Turk, 1995).

It is essential to emphasise here that saying most people with learning disabilities who have unacceptable or abusive sexual behaviours are men is *not the same* as saying that most men with learning disabilities have such behaviours. They do not. Men with learning disabilities have few opportunities to feel good about being men: they may not have jobs, money, relationships or the power which usually goes with being a man in our culture. This book is designed to help the minority of men whose predicament puts them at risk of sexually offending, whether intentionally or not. We do not want it to be used to stigmatise other men with learning disabilities who already labour under considerable disadvantages.

Themes emerging from the work

Here are some points which come up again and again in the course of this workbook:

■ Finding the right words is difficult: how do you discuss the behaviour without either minimising its effects on other people or being too heavy handed?

■ Understanding and trying to explain how a man came to be behaving the way he is can help to put his behaviour into context, but it may not help you manage it in his current service setting: you can sometimes explain his behaviour but you cannot explain it away.

■ If you decide to contain the man's behaviour within the existing service, other service-users or women staff often end up paying the price: how can this be prevented?

■ Sexual behaviour and interests are very difficult to **change**, they need to be **contained** and **managed** instead: base all your planning on the assumption that the man will not change – change things around him to make the service safe for other people.

■ Work out in advance who is responsible for what: do not let the man or the direct care workers in his service fall between several stools.

■ Worry about the basics as well as the specialist input the man needs: step up ordinary processes such as regular reviews, person-centred planning, discussion in staff meetings, supervision of key staff, liaison with family members, reports to care managers or the purchasing agency; do not just rely on one or two hours of therapy or a treatment group – living from day to day is just as important.

How to use this manual

Who is the manual for?

This manual has been written primarily for direct care staff and their managers in services for people with learning disabilities who have responsibility for working with men whose sexual behaviour challenges services or impinges unacceptably on other service-users, staff or members of the public. It is not a book about specialist treatment programmes or about legal complexities. It is a practical book to help you decide whether the sexual behaviour of a man you are working with is abusive or unacceptable, to consider how serious it is and how best to manage it, and to help you co-ordinate services and professional input to support and contain the man in the least restrictive setting which can be made safe.

Structure and design

Mostly, this book is designed to be kept as a reference to be taken down from the shelf and used to guide workers in a particular service as they work together to find shared solutions to problems and safe ways of working with, and for, individuals.

Five **Central Case Studies** are used throughout the text to illustrate the kinds of situations services are facing as well as the strategies that may be put in place to address the men's sexual behaviour. These case studies are based on real people and present a spectrum of the unacceptable and abusive sexual behaviours that services may have to deal with (Thompson, Clare & Brown, 1997). Some changes have been made to preserve the confidentiality of the men and their services. These case studies are italicised and within a border so you can trace the way ideas in the text apply to the situations of these specific men. You will find these **Central Case Studies** on pages 12–13.

Additional scenarios (also in italics) are included at specific points in the workbook to illustrate the potential complexity of situations which may initially appear very similar. Again, aspects of these examples are based on real situations drawn from the research and from our wider experience of men with learning disabilities and their services.

The manual falls into three parts, each of which is organised around three distinct and separate steps:

Part One: The Men's Behaviour

A clear description of a man's sexual behaviour is the starting point for any intervention. This provides a structure for assessment to accurately determine whether a man's behaviour is unacceptable or abusive.

Part Two: Understanding the Men's Behaviour

This identifies what factors may or may not be contributing to a man's abusive sexual behaviour. These factors are the clues to the kinds of responses which will be productive in minimising the risk of further abuse.

Part Three: Service Planning

With the man's behaviour accurately described, and key causative factors understood, the final step is to develop a comprehensive individual service plan.

Photocopiable resources

This part of the book contains all the photocopiable material included in this manual, including the **Activities** and **Case checklists** which are referred to throughout.

Reasons for this structure

In the research project, each of the three stages presented problems to individual staff and to the network of agencies involved in supporting the men. These services often failed to agree:

■ on the fact that the men's behaviour was serious and a problem

■ that there were multiple causes and that the men had experienced many difficulties in their lives which needed to be taken into account in the way their support was arranged and expressed in the level of commitment mobilised for them

■ that consistent steps needed to be taken to protect other people from the men's behaviour and to protect the men from committing offences which might have devastating consequences for them and for others (Brown & Thompson, 1997b).

Why have we tackled it in that order? Well, we believe that you need to start by being clear about what the man is actually doing and on what grounds you are defining it as a 'problem'. You will see that services tend to take a very inconsistent view of sexual behaviour. Sometimes they think it is a problem just because staff are embarrassed or because they cannot help but be aware of behaviour which individual men would prefer to keep private if they could. However, other men are actually committing serious sexual offences and often people continue to act as if their behaviour is not harmful: they may not notice the distress of other service-users or of colleagues; they may discount the seriousness of intrusive behaviour unless it involves members of the public, children or people outside of the services. **Part One** helps you to clarify what is unacceptable and why. It will stop you or others glossing over abuse while also assuring you that you are not interfering unnecessarily. It will help you to document exactly what is happening and who is at risk.

Part Two asks you to step back and look at the man and his background. No one factor causes abuse and we are aware that explanations are sometimes used, not to help with an appropriate intervention, but to let the man 'off the hook'. We do not want to do that. But we do want to look for clues and for ways of helping the men come to terms with the rules of sexual behaviour and appreciate the consequences which may follow if they continue to offend. At the same time we are also aware that many of these men, although they misuse their power in some settings, are generally very disadvantaged, personally, emotionally, vocationally and economically. Looking back over their personal histories allows us to consider a number of factors which may have played some part in the development of their sexual behaviour but it also helps to galvanise some commitment to the men as individuals and to cut across a simplistic view of them as 'baddies' or 'evil'.

Part Three is about planning and it falls into two components:

- firstly (and it is important that it does come first), we are committed to taking proper measures to ensure the safety of others; stopping other people from being hurt is the first step

- secondly, we want to see the men's own lives enhanced and developed. They also have civil rights and entitlements to services and support which we must continue to meet in a humane and supportive way. Our approach is **not punitive**, it is **containing** in that we want to build up those aspects of the man's life which we can support at the same time as we take measures to ensure that his offending behaviour does not continue.

You might find it useful to think of the three stages set out in this manual as being about the *present*, the *past* and the *future*.

Photocopiable resources contains all the photocopiable material included in this pack. Throughout the manual you will find **Activities** and references to **Case checklists** which you can use to help you develop comprehensive individual service plans for men in your own services who may be presenting with unacceptable or abusive sexual behaviour. These could also be helpful to structure discussion at staff meetings, to gain the right professional support and to enlist appropriate mandates from purchasers and commissioners for well co-ordinated interventions.

Activities

A key finding of our research was that the responses to men were determined by a whole set of factors which were not directly related to their sexual behaviour. These included the attitudes and values of staff and carers, the kind of services they lived in, and the ways in which local professionals related to each other. For this reason we have provided activities to help you clarify how these things may be influencing the response your service may be making to men you are responsible for. These may be used as exercises in staff training sessions, to structure group discussions or to precede an agenda item in your staff meeting. If you are working through the manual on your own you can still read through the **Activities** and use the material to structure your thinking and to help you reflect on practice issues.

Case checklists

These are provided to help define and respond to the unacceptable or abusive sexual behaviour of an individual man. They will be useful for you when you need to establish what a man has done, and what factors may be contributing to his behaviour. They also serve as a guide to how to achieve the best response possible within the limitations you will be working under in your own service setting.

The **Activities** and **Case checklists** are included in **Photocopiable resources** at the back of the manual so that they can easily be copied or transferred onto transparencies for use with an overhead projector. They may be photocopied without restrictions.

The Central Case Studies

The five **Central Case Studies** (on pages 12–13) are referred to throughout the book. These case studies have been chosen to illustrate a range of difficult sexual behaviours which face services in relation to men with learning disabilities. By following these same case studies in each of the three parts of the text, we hope to practically demonstrate the process we have worked through and turn your understanding into practical and comprehensive service plans.

Each case study essentially focuses on a specific form of sexual abuse, in terms of the type of behaviour and to whom it is directed. The reality for services is often much more complicated, with men abusing different people in a number of ways, and you will need to 'mix and match' responses to meet the needs of men you work with.

These central case studies are composites based on men encountered as part of the Mental Health Foundation research. They are based on the real histories, living situations and behaviours of a group of ten men we worked with in services in the North East, whose details have been slightly altered to preserve the anonymity of the men themselves and those who have contact with them.

Each of these men is referred to as 'Mr' avoiding the informality of using a first name, or the tendency to see their behaviour as more childish and less serious than that of other adult men. This reflects the seriousness of some of the behaviour the workbook is addressing and also resists a familiarity which often permeates formal discussions and written records of the men's behaviour, such as incident reports and care plans, and which is arguably misplaced in relation to men who are abusing.

We have used initials for the main case studies to avoid the risk of either over- or under-representing cultures which might be assumed from given surnames/ family names. Where culture or ethnic origin might be guessed from a given name, it is not our intention to suggest that certain abusive behaviours are common to a particular culture.

A second way we have used the stories of the men we worked with is as fragments to illustrate particular points or dilemmas. We imagined this as a bit like a kaleidoscope, which when turned and held up to the light rearranged the separate colours and strands in the lives of the men and helped us to clarify the issues. We have presented these fragments as separate scenarios, using first names only. This process may inadvertently make it seem as if we worked with a larger group of men than those we met in the study (Details of the men we met in the study are tabulated in Thompson, Clare & Brown, 1997); it also allowed us to introduce specific examples which we have drawn from our wider practice.

Later sections in the workbook suggest how difficult it is to achieve a consistent account of what has occurred. However, here we are asking you to accept the above case studies as fact. Although limited details are given for each case study we consider that there is enough evidence to label each of the men's sexual behaviour as either unacceptable or abusive. The basis for this judgement will become clear as you work through the materials.

Feedback from the first edition was that *Response-Ability*, being grounded in extensive contact with learning disabilities and services, offered a practical and honest guide in very complex and emotional terrain. We hope this continues to be the case, and welcome comments on this edition of *Men with Learning Disabilities who Sexually Abuse*.

The Central Case Studies

Mr A

Mr A is 22 and lives in a highly staffed group home with just one other man. Because of the severity of his learning disability he never goes out unaccompanied by staff. His sexual problems involve him regularly trying to masturbate in public spaces in the home and day services. He does this by lying on the floor – either inside or outside and moving his hips up and down. Additionally at any time he will be trying to touch his penis and remove it from under his clothing. Because this form of exposure happens when he is being escorted on trips with staff, there is a danger that his access to the community will be further restricted.

Mr B

Mr B, who is 40, also lives in a group home which is staffed 24 hours a day. He is relatively independent and spends a lot of time out by himself. About a year ago a complaint was made to the service about him sexually assaulting a young girl in the local park. The parent who observed the incident from a distance said that Mr B was talking to the child and then he was seen to put his hands up her dress, at which point she shouted at him. He ran away but was identified by another person in the park who knew where he lived. The police were not involved mainly because the girl's mother felt that it would cause the child further distress. In addition to this incident the staff are concerned about Mr B having pictures of children in his room. These are not specifically pornographic, having been collected from TV magazines and other easily accessible publications.

Mr C

Mr C is 32 and is regarded as one of the most able residents living in a large residential service. He has been living there for the past six years. Recently a woman who lived in the same service disclosed during a sex education group at the day service which they both attended that Mr C was her boyfriend and he was 'doing it to her'. She also said 'it hurt when he put it in'. The worker was particularly surprised about hearing this because there was no knowledge of any relationship between the two individuals. In fact Mr C tended to ignore this woman in the course of their activity and work sessions and was very public about having a relationship with another woman who also attended the day centre.

Mr D

Mr D, who is 40, lives in a group home staffed by both women and men. The women staff were complaining that when they were helping him with intimate care he would start to masturbate. Also he would regularly come down from his bedroom early in the morning naked looking for a reaction from the women staff – this did not happen when any of the male staff were on duty.

Mr E

Mr E, who is in his late 30s, lives at home with his elderly parents and attends a large day service for people with learning disabilities. Over the years his sometimes violent behaviour towards other service-users and staff has caused huge problems and he has come close to losing his placement, but the lack of alternative provision has stopped this happening. Recently he was found in the toilets with a very much less able man who has no verbal communication. Clearly there had been some sexual contact between the two. Mr E was unwilling to talk about what had happened and no way was found to establish what the less able man felt about the encounter. On the one hand he did not appear distressed, but on the other, it was known that he would go out of his way to avoid Mr E at the centre.

part
one

The Men's Behaviour

I n responding to men with learning disabilities who may be sexually abusing it is important to establish early on what they are alleged to have done. This process is very difficult not least because most sexual behaviour takes place in private and most people do not like talking about it. So why do labels matter? Until and unless a man's behaviour is clearly defined as a problem, coherent plans cannot be made to supervise him and/or protect others. What happened in the services in Innerborough and Ruralville was that different individuals and parts of the services held varying views of the behaviour and how serious it was. When people failed to clarify *what* had happened the nature and level of response usually depended on *who* it affected. If the behaviour was 'only' affecting other service-users or direct care staff often nothing was done but when, perhaps after many similar incidents which had taught the man that his behaviour would have no consequences, he offended against a member of the public or a child, everyone acted as if this had happened 'out of the blue'. It was as if the service *under* reacted to seriously abusive sexual behaviours when these involved undervalued people and could be contained within the service system, and then risked *over* reacting as soon as they were forced to reckon with the reality of what the man was doing and judge it by the rules and standards which society usually applies to sexual acts and relationships.

A key commitment in the work has to be to reassert the rights of service-users and staff to be protected from sexually abusive behaviour in *all* circumstances and settings, whether this is being perpetrated by powerful men in their families, services or neighbourhoods, or by men who also use their services.

part one

1 First Steps

Investigating – who and how?

Before you sit down to 'interview' a man about his behaviour, or to go over events with someone who has disclosed or witnessed abuse, you must think carefully and consult your manager about whether:

- you are the right person to be conducting this assessment

- your attempt to find out what has happened might cut across any more formal process of investigation

- by asking questions you may be accused of 'coaching' the victim of an alleged incident and inadvertently undermining the actual or perceived integrity of their account

- you might be inviting the man to incriminate himself (possibly falsely) without either you or him weighing up the consequences and risks of his talking to you and perhaps telling you about other things which he might have done.

Do not proceed until you have checked these issues out. Above all you must be clear that you are not investigating the behaviour as a private or personal matter – you have a clear responsibility to act if you discover that abuse has occurred or if you have grounds for thinking that it might do so in the future. You must not give false assurances that you can keep the matter confidential or play 'God' yourself by deciding to overlook an incident or deciding you can contain the behaviour without putting formal plans in place. We make clear throughout this book that enquiry and assessment is part of a longer process which must lead to clear plans being put in place to protect the man himself and other people who are at risk from his behaviour. You need to be sure that you have the mandate on behalf of the service system to take this forward. Getting a clear brief from colleagues in your own and other services will also protect you from any back-biting or concern about your involvement or motives. Lone rangers are not appropriate in this context.

Procedure and process

So do stop and think before you embark on this process:

■ talk to your manager

■ consult the police

■ work within the adult protection policy as set out by your local social services department and any guidelines which exist in your service

■ talk to other professionals who have been involved with the man (such as the local psychology service).

Decide together who is best placed to talk to the man and in what setting. You may decide, for example, to tape the conversation so it can be later transcribed and put on record or to report back within a specific timescale or to a particular meeting.

As we have seen, one important consideration is whether this process may prejudice any subsequent police investigation or criminal prosecution. If there is a reasonable belief that a crime has been committed the police should be notified and consulted immediately. When this happens neither the alleged perpetrator nor the victim should be questioned any further about what took place until a proper decision has been taken about how to proceed and about how to protect everyone's rights.

Policy and partnership – working with the police

Since the publication of *No Secrets* (Department of Health, 2000)[1] social services departments in England must have policies which govern the actions to be taken by different agencies when abuse concerns a vulnerable adult as **victim**. They should appoint someone to co-ordinate the investigation and mediate between the agencies concerned. Increasingly your service will develop policies within this framework for dealing with incidents in which service-users are thought to be **perpetrators** of abuse: work within these guidelines where they exist and if they do not, make a note to feed into discussions after this emergency has been dealt with, so you have sounder structures for making decisions next time. **Part Three** looks in detail at how to maximise the support the police can offer when men with learning disabilities are suspected of sexually abusing.

---

[1] Similar guidance exists in Wales in *In Safe Hands* (The National Assembly for Wales, 2000)

If there are good reasons to believe that the police would have no interest in the incident – perhaps because they would not consider it to be serious enough – the service will need to take matters forward in-house and it may then be necessary to interview the people concerned. However, it is important to be sure that if this is the police response, it is based on a proper appreciation of the situation. You may need to foster better interagency relationships through the multi-agency policy or working group and/or develop links with a designated officer or unit. Be prepared to review your decision not to involve the police if the investigation yields more evidence of sexual abuse than you originally thought.

For the man being investigated, the advantage of a formal inquiry conducted by police is that any interviews will be conducted in the presence of a trained 'appropriate adult' who will work alongside his legal representative and act as a mediator and advocate for him. This protection is based on the conditions set out in the *Police and Criminal Evidence Act 1984* which is designed to provide additional safeguards for vulnerable suspects and witnesses. Its origins are a series of miscarriages of justice involving people with learning difficulties and/or mental health problems who may be more suggestible than others, and who may fail to understand their position within the procedures of the criminal justice system.

If there is an ongoing police investigation, do not talk to anyone connected with the incident without discussing this first with the investigating officers. If someone concerned spontaneously discloses information to you, hear them out and then make a formal record as soon as you can, signed and dated, using their own words as far as you can remember them.

What may happen is that after an initial flurry of activity the police decide to take matters no further and tell you that they are closing their investigation. This should not be regarded as evidence that abuse has not taken place, or a signal that the service need take no further action. Instead it should be seen as the trigger for an intensive period of assessment and consultation within the service network.

See Case checklist A: Starting off

part one

2 Sources of Information

The main sources of information are:

- the man himself
- the alleged victim
- witnesses
- people to whom disclosures have been made
- written records.

Often by checking these different sources very contradictory accounts emerge. This happened quite dramatically in a number of our cases when the assessment process led to very different understandings about what was going on than those initially presented to us. An extreme example was where a day service had named one man as having sexually abused another but when the facts were clear we came to believe that he was actually the victim of the assault.

Talking to the man himself

In work with other sex offenders you might well hold back from challenging the man himself or asking for his account of what has happened. Sex offenders often build up a persona and/or embed themselves in networks which make it extremely difficult for anyone to confront their actions (Waterhouse, Dobash & Carnie, 1994). However, it may be easier to elicit this information from a man with learning disabilities and this presents its own dilemmas. As we work through the examples in the book you will see ways of accessing the man's account of what took place and gaining some insight into his motivation. You will need to decide if this is a viable route to follow depending on the communication abilities of the man concerned *and* your own skills.

You must also build in additional safeguards as you may put the man in a position where he incriminates himself which could have important and unforeseen consequences for him. Other men may be able to censor what they say, or an interviewer may warn them about disclosing previous offences, or get them a lawyer. They will probably know about the system and be able to protect their own rights to some extent and to decide what they say and what they keep to themselves. However, if you are sitting down for a supposed informal chat with a service-user you know and/or have considerable influence or power over, you must work out in advance how best to be fair. If you go into such a conversation angry about what someone is alleged to have done to another service-user or upset about a complaint from a member of the public, you may be tempted to overlook the man's rights but remember you have a duty to him, too (Brown & Thompson, 1997a). If the man has learning disabilities and is formally interviewed by the police, he will be interviewed in the presence of a trained 'appropriate adult' who will protect his rights throughout the process of investigation or assessment (Brown & Egan-Sage, 1996): in informal interviews you must also attend to the man's rights and/or provide an appropriately trained and independent advocate.

Talking to the alleged victim

Similarly, the alleged victim of a sexual assault may be able to provide an important account of what has taken place but another set of considerations needs to be taken into account and very different sensitivities borne in mind when asking them to talk about their experiences. Firstly you must wait until the time is right for them and respect their right *not* to talk to you about what was, for them, a traumatic event. In some cases you will also have to marshal resources and special skills because of the person's communication difficulties or, in the case of children, reasonable concern from their parents about the value and impact of such questioning. You should never make this decision with regard to minors without consultation as you will need to be working within child protection procedures.

You may also need to consider whether the man might have abused, or be currently abusing others and, if so, to trace and talk to these people. You need to think laterally as well as historically to see if there are other vulnerable people who are currently at risk as well as people in previous settings who may have been abused. You may start to see a pattern of disrupted placements or unconfirmed accounts. Services tend to be either blind to the possibility of multiple victims or unwilling to follow up possibilities. It is as if they fear uncovering more abuse.

We met this 'head in the sand' approach in our work. One of the men in the study who had very limited communication skills demonstrated very graphically that he had been sexually abused himself and the signals pointed towards a particular male member of staff. However, the service was unwilling to believe that such abuse was a possibility even though there were ample opportunities for it to have occurred. Because they started from this position they failed to check whether other service-users who were placed in similarly vulnerable positions had experienced similar abuse. It cannot be assumed that people will come forward when they are abused: the dynamics of abuse often include threats and inducements to keep what is happening secret, particularly if there is a marked imbalance of power between the people involved.

Many people who use services and who are asked all kinds of personal questions about their backgrounds do not reveal that they have been abused unless they are asked specifically about it. This gives them permission to speak out and some assurance that they will not get into trouble, or be disbelieved if they do say what has happened. Exploring the possibility of abuse with other possible victims is particularly important when there is concern about other service-users. Placements often put quite able men alongside service-users who are vulnerable on account of physical frailty, profound learning disabilities, sensory impairments and communication difficulties. Quite apart from the need to substantiate what the man was originally believed to have done, being alert to other potential victims is an important starting point for establishing how serious the situation is and what level of support/supervision is going to be needed.

Talking to witnesses

When evaluating accounts from people who have witnessed alleged sexual abuse, it is necessary to recognise that what they see will be filtered by their own attitudes and values. For example, when different staff members found Mr E in the toilet with the other man (see page 13) they took a very different view about what was happening. Some intervened to stop what was going on primarily because of their dislike of men having sex together, while others intervened because they were concerned the sex was not consenting and a misuse of power. Other staff viewed what was going on very positively from their perspective on sexual and gay rights. These conflicting views need to be carefully untangled to provide a useful analysis of the dynamics actually involved.

People to whom disclosures have been made

Like witnesses, people to whom disclosures have been made may also have very different understandings of what they saw or what was said to them. People with learning disabilities report abuse in two distinct ways. The difference is whether they appreciate whether the behaviour is wrong or not. For example, a person with learning disabilities may indicate that a staff member is having sex with them, with or without complaint. Either way, if it is happening, it is serious, and a criminal offence. But people will not always complain when abuse is occurring and conversely, as will be seen below (see **Activity 1e** on page 36), sometimes when people *do* complain, abuse may *not* be taking place.

Written records

Often men with learning disabilities have vague histories with incidents of possible abuse recorded in their case files. Typical of the men whose services we audited were references to 'inappropriate' sexual behaviour going back over a number of years. Such records gave some clues but no firm accounts as to what had actually happened and how it might relate to more recent incidents of abuse. This does not mean that past records should be ignored when you are trying to understand what a man has done and looking for patterns. Instead **they should be read with caution** whether or not they record previous incidents. You must remember how things get missed out and how the author of the records may have fudged or distorted what actually happened.

Remembering historical changes in the way services have addressed the sexual expression of people with learning disabilities is particularly important if you are delving into past files. Blanket prohibitive attitudes to sexuality may have given rise to labels of 'inappropriate sexual behaviour' for contact which was actually consenting, whereas more recent *laissez-faire* attitudes may have led services to assume that sex was consenting when it was not. Incomplete records of past abusive behaviour is most likely when men have abused other people with learning disabilities. It is after all only in the last 15 years that publications have named this as a possibility; previously these incidents would have gone unnoticed and unnoted.

activity 1a   How good is your information?

In your organisation:

1   Are staff:

- negative about *all* sexual contacts including consenting sexual relationships (opposite-sex and same-sex) between people with learning disabilities

- *laissez-faire* in their attitudes so that unconsenting sex may be wrongly interpreted as mutual, or as a relationship?

- careful to distinguish consented from unconsented sex, and mindful of the vulnerability of people with learning disabilities to exploitation?

2   Do clients have 'reputations' which are not supported by documentation?

3   Have past incidents of abuse (or possible abuse) been left unrecorded because:

- abuse would not have been recognised?

- no sexual matters were recorded on people's files?

- the service may have tried to cover up what happened in some way?

- the service was unwilling to record anything which could not be definitely proved?

4   Do individuals and/or organisations use 'confidentiality' as an excuse not to pass on important information about clients you have responsibility for?

See Case checklist B: Collecting information?

part one

Is the Behaviour Abusive or Unacceptable?

This section aims to set out a consistent framework within which to assess the seriousness of the sexual behaviour. Although the law provides some definitions, there is little consensus about the boundaries around what is unacceptable or abusive sexual behaviour for the general population, let alone for the men you are considering. In fact there are few sexual behaviours which everyone would approve of, or universally reject; even behaviours which seem inherently abusive, such as sex with children, are condoned by some people, while legitimate relationships such as sex between consenting adult men are condemned by others. Staff in learning disability services will hold a wide range of views based on their own political, religious and moral understandings. This will be demonstrated in **Activity 1.b**.

activity 1b   Where do you stand?

This exercise works best in a group as it generates lively discussions about people's values and how they have reached their particular point of view. If you are reading the book on your own you can think about where you stand in relation to each statement and perhaps think of the different influences which have led to your views.

Place four large sheets of flip chart paper in the four corners of the room with the following headings on them:

- **Agree**
- **Agree with reservations**
- **Disagree**
- **Disagree with reservations**

continued...

You can put a fifth heading in the middle of the room saying **'Don't know'** or **'On the fence'**.

Then read out one of the statements below and ask each person in your group to stand by the heading which most sums up their view. When they have taken up a position, ask them to look around and find someone with similar views to talk to – give them five minutes to explore why they arrived at the same place. Then ask them to find someone with different views (standing in a different position) and talk to them about why they think as they do. This will allow group members to think about their own, and other people's, views.

You will see that the statements are ambiguous and that group members may confuse:

- their own views and personal/religious values
- their views about what is 'normal' and/or 'typical'
- what is meant by certain words and terms.

Allow people to explore all of these dimensions and reflect these issues back to them as a dilemma and source of confusion. After all, that is the force field within which a staff group has to make its judgements.

Allow ten minutes per item; if you have limited time, select which items you think are useful in your particular service or setting.

The statements

- Whatever consenting adults do in private is their own affair.
- Some degree of violence is acceptable in male-female relationships.
- It is not unusual for women to get hurt during sex.
- Anal sex is quite rightly forbidden in lots of religions.
- Men with learning disabilities should be stopped from doing things which might stigmatise them further.
- Men with learning disabilities should have the same rights as other men when it comes to sexual matters.
- Pornography increases the incidence of sexual attacks and abuse.
- Pornography provides a safe outlet for men who cannot find willing partners.

Defining abuse

So what do we mean by **abusive** sexual behaviour?

Does it always involve a victim?

What if the man does not understand what he is doing?

Is it possible to consent to something which may be harmful?

We are going to work through these issues in stages to help you and your colleagues decide whether individual men you may be working with are sexually abusing. Our definition of sexual abuse covers both contact and non-contact forms of behaviour. Contact abuse involves sexual behaviour where there is physical contact involving sexual parts of the body between the people in the absence of valid consent. This may involve the man touching the other person in some way, or forcing them to touch his own sexual organs. Non-contact abuse includes exposure of genitals or pornography to an unwilling participant and forms of verbal sexual harassment (Brown & Turk, 1992).

Context and consent

You may have noticed that the behaviours happen within different contexts:

- sexual behaviour involving someone else who has not given, or cannot give their consent

- sexual contact with other people with learning disabilities where consent is questioned

- behaviours involving the man alone.

Below we also consider issues of **consent** and of the man's **intent**. All these dimensions are going to be important in unravelling what has happened.

Ann Craft spoke up for the rights of people with learning disabilities, and worked to avoid interference in sexual expression when it was based on the personal, and sometimes capricious, prejudices of workers (Craft, 1994). It is even more important that decisions about what is labelled 'abuse' should be free of bias and arrived at after discussion, and on the basis of agreed and explicit values.

Labelling any sexual behaviour as 'abuse' might seem harsh on men with learning disabilities and many workers hide behind more neutral terms such as 'inappropriate sexual behaviour'. We would argue that while this might be well intentioned it is disrespectful to the people affected by the men's behaviour and ultimately unhelpful to the men themselves, as it serves to mask the seriousness of their behaviour and leaves them open to very negative consequences.

We want to discriminate between:

- actions which are abusive in that they harm others

- acts which are unacceptable or offensive to bystanders or witnesses but which occur because men with learning disabilities, unlike other men, are not in a position to keep their sexual behaviour and interests private

- acts which some might object to, but which are legitimate expressions of sexuality and clearly within the rights of the man concerned.

Without this distinction risks continue not only to other people who may be harmed, but also to the men themselves who may be stigmatised, isolated and unsupported within services on account of legitimate sexual expression which it is their right to pursue as it would be for any other adult.

Consent

We consider sexual abuse to be any sexual behaviour experienced by another person who either has not given their consent or is not in a position to do so because they do not understand or is under too much pressure. A person will not be able to give valid consent if, for example, they are a child, or if they have severe learning disabilities which make an informed choice unrealistic. Our definition focuses on the absence of consent rather than the nature of the sexual behaviour. Some services label or punish men with learning disabilities for engaging in same sex acts simply because it offends their values. This confusion between sexual abuse and consenting sex between men was clear in one group home which prohibited any sex between men on the basis of its Christian philosophy. In such organisations (and there are many) a male victim of a sexual assault is likely to receive the same punitive response as the perpetrator, while men who want to have sex with men are left unsupported and in ignorance of important sexual health issues (Cambridge, 1997, and Thompson, 1994). This is both a neglect of people's rights and a cul-de-sac when it comes to addressing abuse issues.

Individuals differ in their understanding of what consent to a sexual relationship involves. Nowhere is this clearer than in rape prosecution cases where often a woman agreeing to have a cup of coffee in a man's house may be taken as consent to sexual intercourse. The two extreme positions are that consent exists only when it is explicitly given, or that consent is always present unless a person specifically refuses, or is injured resisting. This second understanding is very unhelpful, particularly when applied to people with learning disabilities who for a number of reasons may not refuse sex even when it is clearly exploitative or abusive. Unequal relationships have been identified as 'barriers to consent' in these situations (Sgroi, 1989). It is argued that it is not appropriate to suggest that a person with learning disabilities has given consent to sex with a man with learning disabilities when:

- there is a such a power difference between the two that it precludes consent by the weaker person, for example, if one of them is a care worker as defined in the *Sexual Offences Act 2003*

- there is a significant mismatch between the two people's understanding of the sexual contact, for example, the man with learning difficulties viewing the contact as purely sexual whilst the other person believes that the sex demonstrates a loving relationship

- the value usually accorded to sexual acts is not understood, for example, accepting a cigarette for sex

- the potential consequences of the sexual acts, such as pregnancy or HIV infection, are not understood.

The issue of power

The other major barrier to consent identified with regard to the abuse of people with learning disabilities is the presence of an 'authority' or 'care-giving' relationship such as with staff or within the family and this is stated in the *Sexual Offences Act 2003*. Men with learning disabilities rarely have access to these powerful roles though services used to put service-users in authority over others – a practice which is fortunately dying out.

The legal perspective

Until recently, UK law has failed to provide a useful understanding of consent. This is particularly the case in relation to people with learning disabilities (see McCarthy & Thompson, 2004). The *Sexual Offences Act 2003* addressed many of the previous problems.

The Act states that it is illegal for any sexual touching of a person who has a *mental disorder which impedes choice* if that person:

a) lacks the capacity to choose whether to agree to the touching (whether because they lack sufficient understanding of the nature or reasonably foreseeable consequences of what is being done or for any other reason), or

b) is unable to communicate such a choice, or

c) agrees to the touch because of an inducement offered or given, a threat made or deception, or

d) cannot give valid consent because the other person is a care worker and hence in a position of trust.

With regard to the possible prosecution of men with learning disabilities under any of these conditions, it must also be shown that the individual was aware of the other person's vulnerability.

Other significant aspects of the *Sexual Offences Act 2003* for people with learning disabilities include:

- prohibiting workers and volunteers from having any sexual contact with any person with learning disability to/for whom they provide care, assistance or services

■ extending incest laws to include any sexual relationship with a parent, child, grandparent, brother, sister, half-brother, half-sister, uncle, aunt, nephew or niece. Either person can be prosecuted under these offences which should help address the sexual abuse of adults with learning disabilities by relatives.

activity 1c   Acceptable, unacceptable, inappropriate or abusive?

The following scenarios are designed to help you think about boundaries and imagine how, as a staff team, you can reach consistent and respectful judgements. In each case think about how you would describe the man's sexual behaviour – would you describe it as acceptable, unacceptable, inappropriate or abusive and on what basis would you decide? What are your principles when it comes to deciding which sexual behaviours are OK and can be supported?

Peter

Peter is a man with severe learning disabilities who is regularly found trying to masturbate himself. This can happen anywhere, and staff believe it is because he gets bored. When he masturbates he does not try to involve anyone else – it appears that he just does not understand conventions of privacy very well. When Marie sees Peter trying to masturbate she gently directs him to somewhere private. She remembers having been very shocked to see him do this when she first started working with him, but did not mention it to anyone then.

Keith

Keith is a man with severe learning disabilities who needs help in the bathroom. On a number of occasions he has grabbed the breasts of women staff whilst they were supporting him with his intimate care. New staff are particularly vulnerable to these assaults. There are no similar problems when intimate care is provided by men.

Philip

Philip is very able. In his bedroom he keeps a range of pornography which he has acquired himself over the years. He seems very inquisitive about sex and is often asking the women staff questions which they believe they should answer. However sometimes these questions are very personal, for example 'do you have sex with your boyfriend?' Some staff choose to answer these questions honestly whilst others reply that this is a private matter. One senior member of staff got very angry when he asked about her boyfriend and since that time he has avoided asking her about sex.

Roger

Roger was reported as having been seen masturbating in the bushes of a park by a woman who was passing by. The woman had guessed he came from the local learning disability hostel where she had worked a number of years ago and felt staff should be warned about what he was doing because she believed he might get into serious trouble if someone else saw him.

Intention

You will see that an important feature of our definition is that it does not always hang on the intention of the potential perpetrator – that is, on whether he knew what he was doing was wrong. Whether or not the man *intended* to abuse is a secondary issue and one which should have a bearing only on the interventions around his own behaviour and not used to determine the degree of support given to any victim(s). Even if abuse was not intended, a person who has been subjected to sexual acts to which they did not or could not consent, is deserving of help.

We also challenge the blanket assumption that men with learning disabilities do not mean to abuse. You might think this is harsh because for some men with learning disabilities there are compelling reasons to suggest that their behaviour is innocently misplaced rather than deliberately abusive. Lack of sex education, limited opportunities for acceptable sexual expression and the possibility of the men having been previously sexually abused themselves, are all frequently cited as justifications. Though these are common they do not preclude the possibility that a man might be very conscious that his behaviour is unacceptable. The following factors may be important when deciding whether this is the case:

Targeting the most vulnerable people as victims

If a man with learning disabilities does not know that his sexual behaviour is unacceptable, you would expect it to happen quite indiscriminately – with anyone almost anywhere. This is rarely the case, instead there are often patterns which demonstrate that the man is being selective in his choice of victims.

In the scenarios you considered in **Activity 1c**, Keith has clearly learnt from experience that new staff are 'fair game' for his sexual advances whereas he is more cautious with established staff, some of whom will have found ways to avoid further assaults. Even his apparent lack of interest in assaulting men confirms that he has some control over his behaviour.

Philip is also making choices about who he questions about sex. The fact that he does not ask men suggests that he is less interested in answers than in getting women involved in sexually explicit conversations. Further, his avoidance of the woman staff member who became angry about his questioning indicates that he understood that she did not like his intrusiveness and that his line of conversation is unwelcome.

Other patterns of targeting which can reveal an abusive intent are the consistent choice of victims who are particularly vulnerable. These would include children, less able people with learning disabilities, and people whose physical disabilities limit their chances to escape or report abuse. Confirmation of deliberate targeting may come from the man himself. One man explained that he chose to take a much less able man into the toilets because that man wasn't able to tell staff what was happening to him. He was able to cry in pain when anally penetrated, but not to draw attention to his plight when he was taken out of the staff's earshot.

Hiding the behaviour

People with learning disabilities have good reason to be secretive about their sexual lives because of the pervasively negative reactions they get from services and from their families (Heyman & Huckle, 1995). Therefore many men with learning disabilities will often be reluctant to disclose any aspects of their sexual behaviour – they assume that all sex is wrong and conceal it accordingly. However, where a man is differentially concealing sex which is abusive, for example by putting effort into ensuring his sexual behaviour is not discovered, attempting to silence the victim in any way, lying or denying what is known to have taken place, it is reasonable to assume he has some sense that what he is doing is wrong. What he may fail to understand is how **serious** the behaviour is. For example, Mr C was openly going out with one woman at his day centre whom he referred to as his 'girlfriend' while secretly having sex with, and hurting, a less able woman.

Experience

Is the behaviour experienced as abusive?

Just as abuse cannot be defined only on the basis of intent it cannot be defined solely on the basis of how it is experienced by the more vulnerable person; for example, any adult sexual contact with children is abusive irrespective of how the child experiences it. Society holds this view because we do not consider children to be in a **position** to give informed consent to sex with more powerful adults. Therefore if a man with learning disabilities has any sexual contact with a child it should be regarded as abuse regardless of either the man's intention or the apparent effect of the incident on the child.

If an act *is* experienced as abusive then no matter what the man's intention was or how actively he has sought out the sexual contact, it must be taken seriously. It would be difficult to argue that Peter (see **Activity 1c** on page 30) intended to abuse when he masturbates publicly, but it would be disrespectful towards Marie to deny her distress at **feeling** abused. Her experience might have been as harmful as if an unknown man had intentionally exposed himself to her. Therefore it is important to consider sexual acts abusive if they are experienced as such, irrespective of the motives of the perpetrator. Similarly, regardless of the intentions of Keith and Roger, their sexual behaviour is likely to have been experienced as abusive by the women who were on the receiving end of it. It would be taken for granted that this was the case if they did not have learning disabilities.

So the intention of the abuser and the experience of the 'victim' are both important when making judgements about sexual behaviour which is not consented to by the other person and can be represented in the following chart:

Table 1: Intention and experience of unconsented sex		
Victim's perspective	**Perpetrator's perspective**	
	Intended to abuse	**Did not intend to abuse**
Experienced as abusive	Abuse	Abuse
Not experienced as abusive	Abuse	Unacceptable, but not abusive sexual behaviour

Definitions

ABUSIVE sexual behaviour is something which is *either* intended *or* experienced as an abuse

UNACCEPTABLE sexual behaviour is not intended or experienced as an abuse but one of the parties lacks capacity to consent to their involvement

ACCEPTABLE sexual behaviour is consented to by both parties and neither intended nor experienced as abusive

MENTAL IMPAIRMENT IMPEDING CHOICE: if the act was not intended or experienced as abusive then it could be labelled as unacceptable but should not be stigmatised as abuse

(Adapted from McCarthy & Thompson, 1993)

Using this framework, it may also be possible to shift perceptions: for example, Peter's behaviour (**Activity 1c**) was initially classified as abusive because of Marie's initial reaction to it but Marie now understands that there is nothing personal in his intentions and as a result experiences it differently. However, the service has taken responsibility with her for addressing it and not minimising its effects as a stressful part of her job. In taking the behaviour seriously the service has also considered the effect it has on other service-users who are less able to complain about it. The patterns of behaviour for both Keith and Philip did have an abusive intent and were treated as abusive, even though individual staff members differed in their reactions.

Use **Activity 1d** together with the five Central Case Studies on pages 12–13, which you could photocopy as a handout or write up on a flipchart.

activity **1d**   Abusive or unacceptable?

*Look at the five **Central Case Studies** on pages 12 and 13 and use this model to decide whether you think their behaviour is abusive.*

Case study	Abusive intent?	Experienced as abusive?	Do you think it was abusive, unacceptable or acceptable?
Mr A	☐	☐	
Mr B	☐	☐	
Mr C	☐	☐	
Mr D	☐	☐	
Mr E	☐	☐	

part one

section
4 Consent Issues Between People with Learning Disabilities

One of the hardest challenges for services which recognise both the rights of people with learning disabilities to have sexual relationship and their vulnerability to abuse and exploitation is to make judgments about the acceptability of sexual contacts between people with learning disabilities.

Activity 1e aims to help you clarify the status of sexual activity between service-users and to reach a judgement about whether it is mutual, abusive or exploitative. As we will see, people's personal beliefs about sex can strongly influence their judgements about what is and is not abuse.

One of the factors which makes it difficult to decide what is going on in each of these scenarios is the limited amount of information available to outsiders. It would be useful to know more but the reality is that sexual behaviour is most often conducted in private and people are reluctant to talk about what happens. Too often services respond to this lack of information with an unwillingness to take action. This means that potential sexual abuse, especially of other people with learning disabilities, is left unchecked.

We would argue that there are often clues: the skill lies in making the most of the information which is available and putting together a picture of what has happened in private based on what you know of the two people's relationship in public.

activity 1e   Sorting out consent issues to clarify abuse

Read the following case studies and decide which describe(s) the sexual abuse of a person with learning disabilities?

Do you agree with the staff actions in each of these cases?

Ian and Neil
Staff are surprised to hear some noise in Ian's bedroom. They go in and are shocked to find Ian involved in some sexual contact with Neil, who is 17. They have been living together in the group home for over a year and are thought to generally get on well together. Ian is 29 and the staff tell him he should not be having sex with such a young man.

Michael and Sheila
Michael is found in a quiet corner of a day centre intimately touching Sheila, a less able woman with learning disabilities. She seems comfortable with the contact and is known to regularly seek Michael's attention at the centre which is the only place they meet. The staff's response is to regret that they do not have access to more private space to allow them to enjoy a more satisfying sexual relationship. They choose not to involve Sheila's parents with whom she lives as they believe they would oppose the relationship.

Amir and Billy
Amir and Billy were found sharing a toilet cubicle by staff at a social club for people with learning disabilities. Staff interviewed them alone about what was happening. Whilst Amir says nothing, Billy complains that he did not like Amir touching his 'privates'. In response they reprimand Amir and closely supervise him whilst he is at the club.

Penny
In a sex education group, Penny reveals that her boyfriend, who also has learning disabilities, has sex with her in the grounds of the hospital in which they both live. She says she likes him a lot but that the sex hurts. The group worker is not surprised because she knows that women with learning disabilities often experience sex as painful (McCarthy, 1993) and keeps this information confidential because she considers it to be a very private matter between Penny and her boyfriend.

Key indicators of abuse

We have separated out the key indicators of abuse:

■ use of violence or intimidation

■ different views of what is 'normal'

- different levels of ability

- differences in age

- who takes the initiative?

- the impact of disapproval.

Use of violence or intimidation

It may seem obvious that the presence of violence or intimidation indicates that the relationship is abusive but not everyone will think this. For example, it was only recently recognised that rape within marriage was a crime. Some staff may condone a degree of violence on the part of a man with learning disabilities towards his partners, on the grounds that this is private and the service has no business to intervene. Sometimes workers ignore serious signals, for example, one senior male practitioner dismissed claims that a woman with learning disabilities had been sexually abused despite evidence of scarring on her breast as a result of a severe bite. His assumption was that she enjoyed pain as part of sex even though he had never talked about this with her.

Too often the absence of physical resistance is taken as a sign of consent. It is worth considering how easy it would be for staff to sexually abuse their clients simply by telling the person what to do. This course of action is also possible for relatively more powerful men with learning disabilities who may be willing to use violence to gain the compliance of some people, but do not need to resort to it in order to sexually abuse others.

A man with learning disabilities need not use or threaten violence **at the time of the assault** for it to be a dynamic in the abuse. The victim may have a generalised fear of the man based either on their own previous experience or on having witnessed his behaviour towards others. In one residential setting it was common practice for one resident to lead a much less able man to the toilet. Staff who observed this were well aware that this was about sex and rationalised their lack of intervention on the grounds that the more vulnerable man did not resist. What they failed to consider was how difficult it would have been for the less able man to assert himself with this man whom they themselves were afraid to challenge. Moreover, the man's apparent compliance may have been a strategy to minimise the harm done to him in what was eventually reframed as persistent sexual abuse.

Different views of what is 'normal'

When people are making judgements about sex they are bound to draw on their own experiences and what they consider to be 'normal' or 'healthy'. Penny's physical pain during sex was considered normal so she was not thought to have been abused. Because she did not remonstrate or resist, this was not seen as a serious issue even though compared to the other case studies there were perhaps the most concrete grounds to intervene: it hurt – she did not like it. Over time feminists have alerted us to the pervasiveness of sexual abuse hidden and ignored in 'normal' heterosexual relationships.

Similarly, many services feel more comfortable naming sex between two men as abusive than seeing it as mutually pleasurable irrespective of what is actually going on. This was the case in Ian's and Neil's service (see **Activity 1e** on page 36) which applied a very double standard and was careless of consent issues, being adamant that they would not accept any sexual contact between men, but actively seeking to encourage their male service-users to develop relationships with women.

Different levels of ability

Carers have very different views about the appropriateness of people of different abilities being involved in sexual relationships: from a position which argues that everyone has the right to have sexual relationships to one where certain people with learning disabilities are regarded as too vulnerable to have *any* sexual contact with another person. This continuum was, until recently, reflected in the law which discriminated *between* (and some would say *against*) people with severe, as opposed to mild/moderate, learning disabilities when it comes to consent to sexual activities. But in addition to considering the ability of individuals, it is important to think about the *relative* abilities of the people concerned and the nature of the sexual contact into account.

So although some of the staff team accepted the contact between Sheila and Michael (**Activity 1e**), others argued that the difference of ability made it impossible for Sheila to freely give informed consent to the relationship. Work has shown that men with learning disabilities who have sexual contact with less able people are often dismissive of the possibility of extending this to an emotional relationship because they do not value these people as potential partners. On the other hand less able people may be enthusiastic about having a relationship with a more able man precisely because of their greater status. For them, accepting the sexual contact may be a way of maintaining the association rather than as a way of experiencing sexual pleasure or engaging in a reciprocal relationship.

Services are faced with a similar set of judgements when service-users are involved with partners who do not have learning disabilities. For example:

> **Nigel**
>
> *Nigel was reputed to have had the time of his life with a prostitute who took him away for a weekend and helped him to spend the entire contents of his savings account in three days. His family were furious and the service did have to develop a view about whether this relationship had been consenting on Nigel's part or whether it had been exploitative.*
>
> **Jean**
>
> *Jean went out with a man who was not learning disabled over a period of months and staff were very concerned. Although Jean had only mild learning disabilities, the man intimidated her and had hit her; he took control of her benefits book and tried to stir her up to leave the service. When staff confronted him he said they were 'sticking their noses in' and that Jean wanted to be more independent. Staff felt this relationship was exploitative but felt paralysed to do anything about it until they eventually reported it under the Adult Protection policy and discovered that this man had a previous criminal conviction arising out of a similar situation.*

In all these situations, services can arrive at a supportive, negative or cautious view of the relationship which will inform their interventions. The other stance they can, and often do, take is to opt out and not make a decision. Opting out is almost always the least responsible position.

The new *Sexual Offences Act 2003* gives useful guidance here by saying that it is illegal for people to deliberately target vulnerable people for sexual gain. The people exploiting both Jean and Nigel above could be charged under this new offence. It is important to remember this law could also apply to more able men with learning disabilities. Michael (**Activity 1e**) could be charged if there was a pattern of him taking advantage of someone whose 'mental disorder impedes choice'. This law recognises that some people with learning disabilities may be being exploited even though they are apparently consenting to sex. It is trying to protect people who may know enough about sex to give consent but may not appreciate how they are seen and being treated by another person.

Differences in age

Some sexual acts are clearly viewed as abusive and non-consensual because of the age of the people involved. This is most clear when young children are involved in sex with adult men. It is more difficult to make judgements when one of the people involved is near to, but under, the age of consent, or if there is a significant difference in age between the adults involved. In **Activity 1e**, Neil, at 17, is over the age of consent for sex which is now 16. However, can it be assumed he is being abused or taken advantage of by Ian, who is 29? Even if someone is below the age of consent, services should not make assumptions and staff need an understanding of the dynamics of the relationship. For example, if a man with learning disabilities is egged-on by a group of eleven year old boys to expose himself, the boys are not the victims in this situation; to accept it as such prevents the man from receiving support in this situation.

Hence, although there may be warning bells whenever a man with learning disabilities is having sex with someone where there is a large age gap, this may not necessarily be abusive. Although relationships between wealthy older men and younger women are tolerated (many would say because of sexist and capitalist biases), older men with learning disabilities do not hold this financial power so there does need to be careful scrutiny as to the reasons why a young person may be agreeing to have sex with them, to ensure their naiveté is not being exploited. When men with learning disabilities are having sex with much older people, it is also necessary to ask what the attraction is? It may be that in this case they are exploiting the vulnerability that can be associated with being older, and more frail.

Who takes the initiative?

It is also important to ask who took the initiative, who instigated the sex and who maintains the contact. This will tell you who has the upper hand:

- Was the sexual contact invited in any way?

- Did both people take some initiative for the contact?

- Was one person a passive recipient of the advances of someone else?

These questions will also help you to establish whether the relationship is mutual and reciprocal, or whether a person's vulnerability or compliance has been taken advantage of.

The impact of disapproval

Complaints by service-users about unwanted sexual contact are increasingly taken seriously although they often used to be ignored, but it is important to interpret these against the backdrop of continuing disapproval of sex, and especially same-sex encounters. When Billy (**Activity 1e**) said he did not like the sexual contact, this does not necessarily mean that he was doing something against his wishes. In services where even consented sexual relationships are taboo, if people are 'caught' having sex they might reasonably choose to say they did not like it rather than face the consequences of saying they liked what was happening. This is particularly important to remember when men are found having sex with men.

Ian and Neil

Staff are surprised to hear some noise in Ian's bedroom. They go in and are shocked to find Ian involved in some sexual contact with Neil who is 17. They have been living together in the group home for over a year and are thought to generally get on well together. Ian is 29 and the staff tell him he should not be having sex with such a young man.

Michael and Sheila

Michael is found in a quiet corner of a day centre intimately touching Sheila, a less able woman with learning disabilities. She seems comfortable with the contact and is known to regularly seek Michael's attention at the centre which is the only place they meet. The staff's response is to regret that they do not have access to more private space to allow them to enjoy a more satisfying sexual relationship. They choose not to involve Sheila's parents with whom she lives as they believe they would oppose the relationship.

Amir and Billy

Amir and Billy were found sharing a toilet cubicle by staff at a social club for people with learning disabilities. Staff interviewed them alone about what was happening. Whilst Amir says nothing, Billy complains that he did not like Amir touching his 'privates'. In response they reprimand Amir and closely supervise him whilst he is at the club.

Penny

In a sex education group, Penny reveals that her boyfriend, who also has learning disabilities, has sex with her in the grounds of the hospital in which they both live. She says she likes him a lot but that the sex hurts. The group worker is not surprised because she knows that women with learning disabilities often experience sex as painful (McCarthy, 1993) and keeps this information confidential because she considers it to be a very private matter between Penny and her boyfriend.

In some ways it can be argued that by seeking Michael out at the day centre, Sheila was taking some initiative for the sexual contacts she had with him but this does not equate to her giving informed consent to sex. It can be regarded more positively than if it was always Michael who went in search of Sheila.

The staff person who found Neil in Ian's bedroom was initially concerned about whether Neil was being exploited. However, the fact that the contact took place in Ian's bedroom is significant. They should have asked 'how did Neil get to be in Ian's bedroom? Was he in fact taking some initiative for the contact?' Usually when men with learning disabilities take advantage of more vulnerable people they invade their personal space, for example, by bursting into their bedroom, getting into their bed, or following them into the bathroom.

Similarly, before the staff reprimanded Amir for assaulting Billy they needed to question how he was able to get Billy into the toilet cubicle. If there was no evidence of force, intimidation or learnt compliance, it was reasonable to assume that on some level Billy accepted the contact. The complaint only arose as a result of their being 'caught'.

A continuum of seriousness

As we have seen by examining the dynamics of the contact between the two people with learning disabilities – their relative power and abilities, age and status – it should be possible to reach an informed consensus about the nature of the relationship. Below we describe four points on a continuum which we have found helpful in clarifying what is going on when a man is having sex with another person with learning disabilities. Once you have unravelled the situation and come to a group decision you should be much clearer about what (if any) interventions should be made.

Sexual abuse

Behaviour could be described as sexual abuse when a man with learning disabilities has sex which is either unconsented or where there is no possibility of meaningful consent because of the severity of the other person's learning disability.

Sexual exploitation

Sexual exploitation covers sexual contacts where there are signs that the other person is accepting the sex but there are also concerns that the man is exploiting his greater power over his partner.

Insensitive behaviour

Insensitive sexual relationships are characterised by consent but include sexual acts which are experienced negatively by the man's partner. This may be because the man, or his partner, lacks knowledge about sex, or it may be because he is violent and/or inconsiderate.

Mutual relationships

This is the ideal – both parties want and are consenting to the sexual relationship and it is mutually pleasurable. Mutual sexual relationships may still pose problems to services because of the possibility of pregnancy or sexually transmitted diseases, but the people concerned are well within their rights and deserving of support and information.

Table 2 (page 44) provides a guide to help you decide where you would place a particular sexual relationship between a man with learning disabilities and another service-user. It requires some knowledge of the intentions and experience of both people involved. Later we talk about how to build on your understanding to design an appropriate response. It may be that the relationship crosses over the boundaries between several of these definitions. If this is the case the man's behaviour should be identified by the most serious elements within it. For example, if a man with learning disabilities is having sex with a much less able person the category 'sexual exploitation' applies. However, if this person does not like the man concerned it edges into 'sexual abuse' and the responses made should be more clearly protective of the more vulnerable person.

Table 2: Defining the sexual contact		
Category	**Characteristics of the man with learning disabilities**	**Characteristics of the potential victim**
Sexual abuse	▪ makes threats, uses violence, or intimidates with their strength and/or gender ▪ targets vulnerable people ▪ ignores victim's signs of resistance or pain.	▪ intimidated by or does not like the man ▪ difference in ability which makes consent invalid – especially if the person has severe learning disabilities ▪ distressed by the sexual contact ▪ refused the sexual contact.
Sexual exploitation	▪ makes promises that are not met (for example, 'I'll be your boyfriend') ▪ the only relationship with the person is sex although they are in regular contact ▪ recognises how the sex is for their benefit not their partner's ▪ does not respect or value the partner.	▪ clearly less able ▪ receives money or cigarettes for sex ▪ does not enjoy any aspect of the sexual contact ▪ afraid that the relationship will end if sex is refused.
Insensitive behaviour	▪ lack of knowledge about partner's body and/or their sexual pleasure ▪ difficulties in understanding other people's experience ▪ no attention given to avoiding HIV or unwanted pregnancy.	▪ unaware of potential for their own sexual pleasure ▪ see sex as something they give in return for a relationship ▪ no initiative taken in the sexual contact ▪ accepts anal or vaginal sex as 'naturally' painful.
Mutual relationship	▪ has accurate knowledge of activities their partner does and does not enjoy ▪ shares the initiative ▪ perform similar sexual acts on each other, for example, masturbation or oral sex.	▪ assertive ▪ feels positive about their sexuality ▪ has orgasms.

part one

section

5 'Private' behaviours

Sections **1.3** and **1.4** looked at ways of defining unacceptable or abusive sexual behaviour according to the dynamics between the people involved. Some sexual behaviours which do not directly involve anyone else may also be considered unacceptable. This section looks in detail at what these behaviours might be and at why they present a problem for services. Furthermore, it attempts to set boundaries between what should be regarded as acceptable and unacceptable private sexual expression, thereby ensuring that punitive responses are not made to the men just because they are service-users and unable to conceal their private behaviour. These are delicate judgements and it is important that the views of staff are acknowledged *but* tempered by a commitment to the men's civil liberties. You might find it useful to refresh your memory about the values you debated in **Activity 1b** (page 25) before considering the scenarios in **Activity 1f** (page 46).

activity 1f   Private behaviours

Bill

Bill is a man with severe learning disabilities who is regularly found trying to masturbate himself. This can happen anywhere, and staff believe it is because he gets bored. When he masturbates he does not try to involve anyone else – it appears that he just does not understand the conventions of privacy very well. From time to time staff have tried without success to encourage him to masturbate in a toilet cubicle (they do not suggest his bedroom because it is shared). Now they tend to leave him unless he is outside of his home.

Simon

Simon has always seemed interested in children and collects pictures of them from magazines, picture books and comics which he keeps in a scrap book in his room. Individual work with him revealed that he fantasised about having sex with children and used these pictures to masturbate when he was in his bedroom. This raised great anxiety amongst the staff team although there was no indication that he had ever actually done anything untoward with a child. In response staff took away all of his pictures of children and tried to stop him collecting any more.

Arthur

When cleaning Arthur's room staff found a small collection of women's underwear which had obviously been heavily worn by him. They could not work out where he had acquired them – he did not have the skills to buy them from a shop and he would not say anything when they asked him about them. For so called 'hygienic' reasons they threw them away, without telling him.

Paul

Paul is known to play with his faeces when he is in the toilet. This has happened for many years and no one is sure why he does it – he says he gets 'a nice feeling'. Staff have continually tried in different ways to discourage him from this habit. The current strategy is to heavily prompt him to do the clearing up which is necessary after his activities.

Ivan

Ivan has severe learning disabilities. He tries to find objects to stick up his rectum when he is alone in his bedroom. The staff worry about what damage he may do to himself, and are very careful not to leave likely objects lying around and to check his bedroom at night times. However this is an uphill struggle and most mornings there is evidence that he has used something – often pens, pencils or cutlery.

continued...

- Which of the above sexual behaviours would be regarded as unacceptable in your service?

- Do you agree with this definition?

- Do you agree with the actions staff have taken in each case?

What's the problem?

In all the scenarios in **Activity 1f** staff have taken action to prevent some aspects of the man's sexual expression – behaviour which is for his sole pleasure, and in which he does not seek to involve anyone else. We see that in some cases the man does not know how to be private but in others his sexual interests come to light because of the abnormal access which staff have to *his* private space and because they consider themselves to have a mandate to scrutinise his behaviour.

Staff understandably respond to sexual behaviour when they stumble across it. Although it is part of the job and experienced workers might become quite blasé about it, we should remember how extraordinary the work is. Young staff would not encounter these things if they worked in an office, a shop, a garage or a factory. Staff may be offended, embarrassed and/or disapproving. They may intervene without even justifying their reactions, or they may come up with excuses which really do need to be unpicked. What are the grounds for disapproving of these acts and how reasonable are they, for this man and in these circumstances?

Privacy

It is generally accepted that sexual activity should take place in private, that is, it should not be witnessed by people who have not chosen to be involved. This is why staff try to prevent Bill (**Activity 1f**) masturbating where he may be seen by other people. However, their actions reveal that they adjust their notion of privacy depending on who is witnessing the behaviour. They stop him masturbating in public but tolerate his behaviour if it is in front of staff. He shares a bedroom and it is likely that his roommate is also exposed to it regularly and without intervention. Thus we see that his behaviour is treated differently when there is a risk that it will be seen by any member of the general public but tolerated when it is in front of other people with learning disabilities or staff. Of course this double standard is not right, but it is a very typical compromise.

It can be difficult to help men with severe learning disabilities to understand and conform to rules about privacy but it is important to separate the effect of the man's cognitive difficulties from the way his learning is undermined by aspects of his care. For example, if a man resides in a service which consistently fails to address public masturbation or which does so inconsistently there is little chance that he will acquire the concept of privacy, or learn to keep within it.

But men with learning disabilities have far *fewer* opportunities for privacy with regard to their sexual behaviour, so staff do have to be sensitive to, and respectful of, their attempts to keep their sexual behaviour private. For example, the contents of their bedrooms are often 'policed' by staff and other carers – if Arthur did not have learning disabilities it would be much easier for him to conceal items of women's clothing. Similarly, without learning disabilities there would be less chance that Simon would have revealed his sexual interest in children, and Paul would be more able to clear up the signs of his playing with faeces. Because of this atypical access to the private sexual behaviour of men with learning disabilities, there should be great caution before describing the behaviour as 'weird', 'unnatural' or 'deviant'; other people are able to find ways of keeping aspects of their sexuality hidden. Nonetheless the very fact that staff do know about these things puts them in a position where they have to take a view about these issues.

Wrong time, wrong place

While not directly criticising the nature of the sexual behaviour, staff may raise objections to the time and/or place in which it takes place. This is a frequent concern in day centres where staff often argue that because they function as a place of work, service-users should not be engaging in sexual behaviour. Such criticism tends to overlook the possibility that staff may themselves be masturbating in the toilet unproblematically. One option in these situations is to encourage men with learning disabilities to differentiate between work and break times with regard to the times they may choose to masturbate. With less able men who have a poor concept of time it may be more pragmatic to allow them the opportunity to masturbate privately as and when they choose, but at the same time reflect on whether the work activities offered lack interest for the man, and need changing.

Health risks

Another reason why services may feel compelled to intervene is out of concern for the man's or for other people's health. For example, the worries about the consequences of Ivan inserting objects in his anus, or the risks to Paul or other people who use the bathroom which will arise if they have contact with his faeces[1].

---

1 Smearing of faeces could actually be a sign of anal masturbation (stimulation of the prostate gland). This often occurs when the man is unable to masturbate his penis – possibly because of the side effects of medication.

Though these risks are undeniable, it is important to recognise that other men are able to engage in similar activities while safeguarding themselves from any adverse effects to their health. Therefore staff have to work out whether it is more appropriate to put energy into reducing the health risks rather than preventing the sexual activity. In the scenarios described above, this could mean providing Ivan with a safer object to use, or diverting energy from stopping Paul to concentrating on his skills in cleaning himself and the bathroom after his activity. Potentially these strategies may be more productive not least because his behaviour takes place privately which reduces the possibility of consistent behavioural intervention. This harm minimisation approach is also more respectful to the man's choice of sexual expression – whatever that is.

Disapproval

Although health concerns may be presented as the reason why staff are unhappy about a particular behaviour, they may be masking a basic unease about what the man is doing. Many staff will find it unpleasant to know that a man with learning disabilities plays with his faeces, or inserts objects in his anus, aside from any unease they may feel in having to confront the physical evidence of these activities (ie the objects or unclean bathroom). Whether such cultural disapproval of the man's activities is enough to lead to regarding them as unacceptable needs to be questioned. For example, the response to men with learning disabilities found simply masturbating in private has often been one of reprimand. Although such disapproval is more often tempered there are many staff, often supported by their own beliefs, who would hold that such behaviour is inherently wrong. However, sexuality policies have to start from a sexual rights perspective and support staff in *not* acting on the basis of their 'gut reactions'. So staff should be cautious about trying to stop men with learning disabilities simply on the basis of their personal feelings. Services have a duty to uphold the civil liberties of men with learning disabilities in relation to sexuality as well as other areas of their lives.

Unfortunately professionals are not always careful to make this distinction, and will try to stop certain sexual activities because they simply do not like them rather than because they have an effect on other people. For example, one study included a man with learning disabilities in a programme for men who sexually abuse simply because he enjoyed wearing women's clothing (Day, 1994).

Perhaps this kind of disapproval underpinned the decision to remove Arthur's collection of women's underwear but the staff have to question the extent to which they should be 'policing desire' (Watney, 1989). The underwear may have been dirty, but this was really a pretext and could have been solved by providing him with an opportunity to use the washing machine. The items may have been stolen, but he could possibly have acquired them from a legitimate source. The acceptability of pornography in private needs to be considered in a similar light.

There are feminist campaigns to ban its availability – generally because of its links with sexual violence (Dworkin, 1981) – but it is questionable whether this gives services a mandate to stop men with learning disabilities from using it, when so many other men do.

It really should not matter what staff think about what men with learning disabilities do in private, their job is to act respectfully to them and to support their choices as long as the men are not harming other people or themselves.

Concern about risk of sexual assault to others

It is likely that staff would regard Simon's masturbation to images of children as indicative that he might go on to abuse children, so that in addition to their understandable discomfort at having to acknowledge his fantasies, they need to decide how great this risk is. Although removing the pictures might seem like a constructive solution there is no evidence to say that this will be safer than allowing him to keep the materials. It is possible that assaults have been avoided because he has access to them. Services which have tried to prevent men with learning disabilities from keeping pictures of children have found it an uphill struggle, and there is a danger that by encouraging the man to resort to underhand tactics to conceal his continued use of the material, you undermine the possibility of honest discussions with him about his behaviour.

The staff's decision may be taken on the grounds that he has not committed any assaults against children and in acknowledgement of the extreme difficulty of changing sexual interests. This is *not* an argument for casually accepting masturbation to images of children but an expression of the need at certain times for services to tolerate it within tightly controlled boundaries. The service would need further assessments to be carried out. They will not be able to manage the anxiety of allowing him to continue unless they are sure they have put structures in place and that they have the support of other professionals and their managers. This is a good example of the containing approach we wish to advocate in this book. Blaming often leads to punitive attitudes and to isolation but it does not work to stop assaults. Acceptance and awareness may allow more robust safeguards around a man which paradoxically also allow him more freedom because the service is **actively working with him** to prevent him from committing an offence.

Respecting diversity and the men's best attempts to be private

Services need to be careful about responding to private sexual behaviour as if it were automatically unacceptable. There needs to be clarity about exactly what the problem is, if any, and for whom? It is likely that men without learning disabilities engage in a similar range of behaviours without interference from other people. Increasingly agency policies are being adopted which enshrine respect for sexual diversity and which set up structures for individual care planning and shared decision making in the face of risk. These obviate the need for staff to respond as individuals, but also act to limit their freedom to interfere in the private sexual behaviour of others just because they disapprove themselves.

See Case checklist C: Recording the behaviour

part
two

Understanding the Men's Behaviour

In **Part One** we tried to help you arrive at a clear picture of the man's unacceptable or abusive sexual behaviour – of *what* he is doing. In this part of the workbook we will focus on *why* he is behaving like this. By exploring the roots and meaning of the abusive behaviour you will be in a better position to identify a care plan which can address and contain it. You may also find it easier to work alongside and respect the man even if you do not like what he is doing.

Whatever framework we use to gain an understanding of sexually abusive behaviour we must also maintain a certain degree of scepticism – the motivations for any human behaviour are too complex to be reduced to a handful of statements about the person. In many ways the hypotheses you build up are always going to be guesses but the aim is that they should be well informed guesses, rather than unchallenged or discredited assumptions.

Moreover, working out *why* is only an intermediate step – it does not necessarily tell you *how* to change or manage the behaviour. Our experience is that services often stop when they think they have understood, as if that were the end of the matter. All their energy goes into trying to make sense of the behaviour, rather than into working together on how to contain it and minimise its damaging consequences. At worst some kinds of explanations seem to 'excuse' the behaviour; at best, you might find it easier to support the men as individuals when you appreciate their own difficulties.

Go to Activity 2a: Understanding the men's behaviour

part two

1 Different Kinds of Theories

The men's stories we encountered during this study raise fundamental questions about how we believe sexuality and sexual behaviour develop and are shaped. Is it all innate, determined by our genes, and 'natural', with society's rules there to keep it in control? Or is it learned as a result of watching adult role models or peer group pressure? Are we moulded by advertising or by the images we see around us in films and on television? What affect do society's rules about sex, as these are taught through religious and moral education, have on individual behaviour?

What is 'theory' anyway? You often hear someone say 'well that's all right in *theory* but we have to work with this man...' or 'well that is just *theoretical*'. We often talk about the need to turn **theory** into **practice**. These snippets remind us that theory is one step removed from the immediate situations. It provides a 'model' about why things happen, and often comes couched in its own jargon or special language. Some of these languages are very difficult for an outsider to understand, so, instead of helping, the theory can make things seem more difficult.

Many theories are developed within particular 'disciplines' and professional groups which focus in depth on one part of the picture instead of how they all come together. For example:

■ a psychiatrist may explain how a particular medical condition or mental illness could affect someone's sexual behaviour

■ a behavioural psychologist would look at how a man's behaviour has developed and been shaped by the responses of others

■ a cognitive psychologist would focus more on whether the man has distorted thoughts about sex, and

■ a psychodynamic practitioner would look at his internal emotional world and landmarks in his personal history.

They would constantly be testing out their ideas and developing new ones through research and analysis of their clinical practice. Other disciplines focus more broadly on the way society and its institutions are organised, or on culture and the way imagery and marketing influence our perceptions and ideas.

Any, or all, of these approaches might give you valuable insights about a man you are working with. We have found them all valid ways of looking at the problems the men have experienced themselves and are now presenting to others. The approach we take is called **eclectic**, because we draw on all these types of thinking. We found practitioners we spoke to in the course of this study were more alert to some theories than others; for example, most people had heard of the idea that if someone is sexually abused and not helped to get over it they may go on to abuse others but few were aware of the research which links sexual abuse with isolation, loneliness and disrupted attachments. The reviews by Brown & Thompson (1997c) and Lindsay (2002) provide helpful summaries of the research on men with learning disabilities who sexually abuse.

In our study few services had consulted specialists about the impact of particular medical conditions, including genetic syndromes, mental ill-health and side effects of medication, or were alert to these as a possible source of difficulties. For each man, we recommend you 'knit' together a number of relevant theories, seeing how different factors have interacted, how a man's experience may have influenced his learning and thinking, and how wider structures such as changing service provision have disrupted his life or distorted his social networks. In trying to understand as fully as you can, move back and forth between his inner world and external realities – between the past and the present.

Sometimes you might find that 'experts' argue in favour of their own and against another person's way of understanding. They may be very persuasive. You should be assertive in asking them to translate their special knowledge into a useful set of ideas for you. If you do not understand what they are saying it is not because you are not clever enough, or because that approach is not relevant – it is more likely that the person has not made the shift from talking in their own language, within her or his profession, to talking to people outside it. They need to **translate** their way of looking at problems. Increasingly this is being seen as a vital skill and prerequisite of multi-disciplinary working. Men with unacceptable or abusive sexual behaviours are going to be some of the most complex to understand and work with: they, and you as the people directly managing their behaviour, are entitled to the input of specialists to help you limit the damage they may otherwise do to others and to themselves. Do not let yourself be talked down to. Good theories make things simpler to understand, not more complicated.

You will see that these theories often look at different layers in someone's life, from a little part of them like a gene, or biochemical imbalance, to the way they interact with others, to their biography, and then to their wider environment. Sobsey (1994) called this an 'ecological' model and visualised it as a series of concentric circles within which the individual and their abusive behaviour is located.

We are all familiar with the sayings 'we are our history' and 'we are products of our environment'. We also know that learning disability sometimes has social origins and that a difficult start in life can disadvantage someone throughout their adulthood. By separating these areas out we are trying to unravel the different factors so you can see each strand separately before knitting them back together.

When you come to use this section to explore the possible origins of the behaviour of a man who is sexually abusing in your own service, you will need to draw up your own list of possible 'factors'. For each man there will be a number of relevant and often overlapping ideas, and it is helpful to avoid statements like 'the behaviour is caused by the fact that he had an abusive childhood' or 'he abuses because he cannot find a willing partner' – rarely, if ever, will there be one simple cause or such a degree of certainty.

part two

section
2 The Men's Life Stories

You may want to look back to the **Central case studies** on pages 12–13, to see what you already know about the men, before we turn to them again, adding in more biographical details to illustrate these points. You may find some of these stories very depressing as we did throughout the research study. It was commonplace for the men we met to have had:

- little control over where, or with whom, they live

- previous long-term placements in large institutions or other residential accommodation

- a disturbing lack of continuity in their lives as they were moved from one service to another

- few lasting relationships with family, friends or past carers.

Such experiences are typical of the lives of many people with learning disabilities, not only those who present with abusive sexual or other challenging behaviours. But do these upsetting histories provide clues as to why the men are now sexually abusing? As you read the men's stories you might find it helpful to make a note of the factors which you think may be contributing to their abusive or unacceptable behaviour.

Mr A

At about the age of seven, Mr A was moved from his home city to a residential school in the country. Little is known about his life before then. He returned to the city just two years ago when he was twenty because the school was closing down. During the transition period, staff from the new group home visited the school and saw he was the only black man in the school. They also remembered the poor priority given to privacy and dress – Mr A never wore shoes and they saw other people walking around in even greater states of undress without gaining the staff's attention. No one from that time in his life is still in contact with him, including his family. Although it is clear that he has preferences amongst the people with whom he shares a service and the staff, he is not thought to have any particularly strong friendships.

Mr B

Mr B lived with his mother until he was found in their flat one day with her dead body – the flat was in a disgusting condition with faeces spread all around the rooms. He had not had contact with services before then and neighbours at this time reported that he used to roam markets with his mother collecting food discarded by vendors. At that point he entered learning disability services and was moved to a local hostel. This was ten years ago when he weighed just forty-five kilograms (seven stones). At the hostel they had several problems with his sexual behaviour, including him stripping naked by a window, gesturing masturbation to the neighbours, smearing faeces and urinating in public. The most serious incident occurred shortly after he arrived at the hostel when he started to take his penis out in public and thrust himself against a girl of 12 who was passing. For a while after this incident it was decided that Mr B should not go out unaccompanied. This arrangement had lapsed by the time he moved to a nearby group home when the hostel closed three years ago. He has been diagnosed by a psychiatrist as having hypomania and two years ago spent a short period in a psychiatric hospital which he did not enjoy. His physical condition is very much improved and he is no longer underweight.

The group home attempted to make links with his family and found his brother who showed no interest in re-establishing a relationship. Mr B had a couple of good friends at the hostel but they moved to other areas when it was closed down and he has not had any contact with them since that time. Otherwise the only people he names as important to him are the current staff of the group home. He still thinks a lot about his mother and the neighbourhood in which they used to live together.

Mr C

Four years ago Mr C moved from his family home to the local residential service. He still has regular contact with his family – mainly his mother and older brother who still lives at home. These people are very important to him and he is with them most weekends even though his violent behaviour at home was the main reason for his admission to the hostel. About ten years ago suspicions were raised that Mr C had been abused physically and maybe sexually by his mother's boyfriend at that time although nothing was proven and no action was taken. Other concerns about his family life have been raised over the years, most recently that his brother lets him view very explicit pornography, and shares with him some very negative attitudes towards women.

Mr D

Mr D was born 40 years ago, and early on was diagnosed as having Marfan's Syndrome. His mother felt unable to take him home so he was admitted to a children's home. One of the staff members there took a particular interest in him and has remained in contact since that time though this is limited to sending him birthday and Christmas cards. At the age of 12 he was admitted to a large hospital for people with learning disabilities because the home was finding him increasingly difficult to manage. He stayed at the hospital until it closed 25 years later when he was moved to his current group home. There was no mention of sexual problems at the hospital or in his records, although during the admission process they said that he had occasionally exposed himself and invaded other people's privacy. Soon after moving to the group home major sexual problems surfaced, in particular exposure to women staff (which was written off as 'institutional behaviour').

The staff member from his previous children's home is the only contact who kept in touch after his two moves, firstly to the hospital and more recently to the group home. He has special relationships with some women staff although these are the ones he singles out for unwanted sexual attention. He has often talked about getting a girlfriend and is reported to have behaved like a 'proper gentleman' once when he invited a woman to dance whilst on holiday.

Mr E

Mr E was born in the early 1960s and has been diagnosed as having Prader-Willi Syndrome (a chromosomal disorder), the effects of which include a tendency to obesity and undeveloped male sexual organs. It is believed that he has some understanding of his condition and is self-conscious about his 'differentness'. He is very aware of the difference between his penis and those of other men. He continues to live at home with his mother and father who are very active in the local parent support group, as well as in the Prader-Willi association. For a brief period in his 20s, Mr E lived in a group home but his parents withdrew him because he was gaining weight. They felt staff were unwilling to take the necessary responsibility for carefully controlling his diet.

On a number of occasions he has become very emotionally attached to women staff members, seeking them out and becoming painfully upset in their presence. His relationships are primarily with his family and staff, although he has also spoken positively about a sexual contact that he had with another male service-user at the day centre.

part two

3 Unravelling the Causes of the Men's Behaviour

In trying to understand the men's behaviour we looked again at our main case studies, including their:

- physical development and medical histories
- current mental health and use of medication
- understanding, knowledge and learning from previous incidents
- masturbation, sexual fantasies and use of pornography
- cultural factors
- personal and family relationships
- current relationships, social networks and service settings.

These layers of their past and present lives are heavily inter-related. Using diverse theoretical positions we began to explore the impact of these men's past and current relationships and settings.

Physical development and medical histories

We had not expected to find that medical factors played a significant part in the development of the men's behaviour and approached this task thinking that we would find their personal histories more relevant. Only a minority of people with learning disabilities can trace their impairment to a specific medical condition such as Down's Syndrome (which is chromosomal), cerebral palsy (which is often caused by lack of oxygen during birth), or brain injury for any reason at or around birth. Medical factors are rarely cited as explanations of the sexually abusive behaviour of men in the general population and we do not want to provide an easy answer to a complex question.

We are therefore cautious about overstating their significance for men with learning disabilities who sexually abuse.

The research we did was 'qualitative' which means that we looked at a small number of men in depth: this is often useful to find out what the issues are in a previously under-explored area of work. Such research, because it is entered into with an open mind, is useful for identifying what the key questions might be rather than necessarily finding answers. If we wanted to find out whether men with specific impairments were more likely to develop difficult sexual behaviours we would need to design a different kind of study which could look at a larger group of men and make this comparison. Here we are just stating that this is an issue worth exploring in relation to the men you are concerned about.

Amongst the men studied in the case studies both Mr E and Mr D were identified as having specific impairments – Prader-Willi and Marfan's Syndromes respectively. Having little knowledge of these we turned to direct support staff, community nurses and psychiatrists for information. We also wrote to a consultant geneticist and used a medical library. This is what we found out[1]:

Marfan's Syndrome is a genetic condition whose key feature is long bones which makes people with the syndrome very tall. Other features are heart and eye problems. There is no indication that sexual development is affected. Intelligence is also believed not to be affected, which means the syndrome itself does not explain why Mr D has a learning disability.

Prader-Willi Syndrome is also a genetic condition. In adults it is associated with severe obesity which is linked to a failure of the body to chemically register when enough has been eaten. The sexual organs do not develop fully. For men this means that the penis is small, the testes do not descend and there is sparse pubic hair. There is no evidence of men with Prader-Willi having had children. Unlike Marfan's Syndrome, it is likely that people with Prader-Willi will have a learning disability.

We also researched Down's Syndrome because it is the most commonly identified syndrome amongst people with learning disabilities:

Men with Down's Syndrome have normal looking genitalia, that is penis and testes size, and pubic hair, but they may experience difficulties with erection and ejaculation. Men with trisomy 21 are usually sterile although rare exceptions have been reported (Sheridan *et al*, 1989). This contrasts to women with Down's Syndrome who have a reduced, but significant, fertility.

---

1 The main papers we looked at were Laurance (1993) and Pyeritz & McKusick (1979).

These conditions have impacted on the men we were concerned with:

Mr E is not able to masturbate as other men do, and this will also be the case for many men with Down's Syndrome. As we saw in Part One, staff often have a lot of knowledge about the private sexual behaviour of men with learning disabilities because of the intimacy of their role. It is, therefore, worthwhile asking them what they have observed so that the men can be offered appropriate support. Staff we spoke to about these men were able to confirm that Mr D was capable of both erection and orgasm, but no one had ever seen Mr E with an erection. This did not mean that he could not or did not have any sexual pleasure because on one occasion he had been found pressing an electric toothbrush onto his genital area.

Explicit discussions with Mr E were helpful in allowing us to empathise with his understanding of the fact that he had underdeveloped sexual organs and how this impacted on him and on his behaviour. He said he liked looking at pictures of penises in magazines which he bought. There could have been a number of reasons why he said this but it did suggest that he was aware of the fact that his penis was unusually small. This had been suggested in a psychological report made over ten years previously which said that he was 'conscious of his undeveloped male sex organs and unable to accept and deal with this problem'. This report sounds rather clinical (in the worst sense of the word), a bit cold and unsympathetic, when what is being said might be a very understandable emotional response to the appearance and limited function of his genitals.

As Marfan's Syndrome does not affect the sexual response system we were no closer to understanding Mr D's behaviour. However, like Prader-Willi it does mean that Mr D has somewhat unusual physical features, being abnormally tall and thin, which marks him out as 'odd' in his local community and means that he tends to be stared at whenever and wherever he goes out.

The physical manifestations of these men's syndromes seemed to have contributed to generalised low self-esteem for both of them. Mr E's appearance was very unusual because of Prader-Willi Syndrome and similarly Mr D's was typical of men with Marfan's Syndrome. Mr E was the most clear about not liking the way he was – particularly the underdevelopment of his sexual organs, but also his weight. We know how common it is for people to suffer great anxiety because of their weight – so it is reasonable to speculate that men with learning disabilities may be similarly emotionally affected by their appearance. Aside from physical appearance, standard of dress and cleanliness has a bearing on a person's self-esteem. Too often people with learning disabilities have little control over these areas, being dependent on the care of others to ensure that these issues are appropriately attended to.

There are a small number of cases written up where sexually abusive behaviour has been attributed to another specific condition – Klinefelter's Syndrome (Lachmann *et al*, 1991; Raboch *et al*, 1987; and Hummel *et al*, 1993) which is a genetic variation sometimes associated with learning disability. However, the evidence for this is contested and some studies have found that men with Klinefelter's Syndrome are less sexually active than their peers (Raboch *et al*, 1979; Sorensen, 1992). Other syndromes which effect hormone levels may also be linked to abusive behaviour, although again the evidence is contradictory as to whether testosterone levels are directly related to how sexually active men are (Wilson & Foster, 1985).

This section should not lead you to think, 'Oh well, Mr X has such a syndrome which explains his behaviour. There is nothing we can do'. This is stigmatising and simplistic. However, it might help you to understand and support an individual man if you can find out just exactly how he might be affected by his condition. You could talk to him to see how far he is aware of these difficulties, and how he feels about, and/or manages them. Talking with a man in an honest way may provide him with a unique and sympathetic opportunity to share how he feels, to have his concerns validated and to break a painful taboo by acknowledging his physical characteristics.

Current mental health issues and use of medication

Other physiological conditions have also been cited as issues related to difficult sexual behaviour, including traumatic brain injury which may sometimes lead to an individual's placement in learning disability services. Problems with the structure of the brain have at times been linked to unacceptable sexual behaviour, though rarely with serious sexual offences (Verberne, 1990). These include permanent brain damage, tumours (Lisman, 1987), and temporal lobe epilepsy (Bear, 1984; Lisman, 1987). None of these factors were present for any of the men in our study. Where they do have an impact it is usually related to disinhibition – a common consequence of acquired brain injury. The theory is that parts of the brain which control impulses and desires are either underdeveloped or damaged. This reflects a perspective that all men have the potential to sexually abuse, but most are able to **control** their impulses. This does not necessarily mean that they draw on a conscious **morality** to stop them abusing but that they calculate the consequences of such actions. For example, almost half of male college students in one study said that they would sexually abuse women if they believed they would escape prosecution (Boeringer, 1996). This suggests that men's self regulation relies more on the awareness of potential consequences for themselves rather than fear of the harm to any potential victim.

There are also strong grounds to make links between specific mental health problems and men's sexually abusive behaviour[1]. This was the case for Mr B who received a diagnosis of hypomania (a form of depression) after incidents of sexually abusive behaviour. He was treated with thioridazine – a major tranquilliser: the dosage being adjusted on a number of occasions to reflect his sexual behaviour at the time.

It is very common for men with learning disabilities who have sexually abused to have been diagnosed with mental health problems and to be taking some form of psychotropic medication. Two studies found that mental health problems were present in one third to one half of men with learning disabilities who had sexually abused (Day, 1994; O,Connor, 1994). However, men with learning disabilities may be taking psychotropic medication long after their symptoms have abated; in some services over-medication is routine and in others there is a failure to review long-term medication on a regular basis. Therefore, it should not be assumed that abusive behaviour can be directly explained by mental health problems even when a man is on psychotropic medication. This may become apparent if treatment fails to alter the abusive behaviour.

Some of the practitioners in this study took a cautious approach to too easily attributing sexually abusive behaviour to mental health problems. They said they were afraid to refer men to local psychiatrists because they did not want the problem medicalised, with the result of the men being prescribed psychotropic drugs or being hospitalised. Obviously this does not point to healthy relationships between professionals or good multidisciplinary working. These tensions exist in many services and have a negative impact on the treatment of men with learning disabilities who sexually abuse. However, we should also add that other practitioners we met spoke very positively about the input and support they had received from psychiatrists and regarded the mental health system as supportive when it came to diagnosing the men's difficulties and planning around containment and treatment.

Mental health problems may affect sexual behaviour in a number of different ways. They may produce disinhibition alongside the conditions cited earlier, but also lead to a man acting out delusions. More recently links have been made between depression and sexually abusing behaviour. One hypothesis is that a man who is depressed may feel so bad about himself that he may care little about the possible consequences of sexual abuse for himself and hence fail to regulate his behaviour. This theory has led to anti-depressants becoming a primary treatment for some men in the general public who sexually abuse.

---

1 For a description of a man who acted out hallucinations of sexual abuse see SM Sgroi's chapter 'Evaluation and treatment of sexual offence behaviour in persons with mental retardation'. In Sgroi (1989), pp245–283.

Low self-esteem, arising from emotional isolation or depression has also been linked to a wide range of concerning behaviours. Within the case studies, low self-esteem was most evident in Mr B's case. It could be seen in his passive acceptance of the restrictions and changes forced on him by services. Although he knew that the police would be involved in any further incidents of sexual abuse, and that detention in a psychiatric hospital would be a likely outcome, it was felt that these were ineffective deterrents for him, even though he had previously experienced both interventions and not liked them. The staff who worked with him considered that he did not place any significant value on where he lived or what happened to him. This was evident when he was asked about whether he would mind if staff insisted that he did not go out alone: his answer changed frequently but what was consistent was his lack of concern. In one case conference Mr B was asked where he was happier living – the current group home or the closed hostel. Mr B answered twice, contradicting himself. His demeanour suggested that he did not expect his opinion would be listened to or respected. It is not surprising that Mr B had reached the conclusion that he has no control over what happens to him, for this has been his actual experience. He did not have a say when he moved away from the area he loved after his mother died, and neither did he have a say in whether he wanted to move from his previous hostel – it closed.

For individuals who are identified as having low self-esteem, deterrents may actually be counter-productive when trying to reduce abusive behaviour. The person may view the deterrent as confirmation of their lack of worth, rather than as something to be avoided. This does not mean that knowledge should be withheld about what may happen as a result of further abusing – whether or not Mr B is able to take responsibility for the consequences of his actions he should at least be informed of what these might be.

Few people with learning disabilities drink alcohol or use other 'recreational' drugs but these may be possible factors in understanding the behaviour of some men with learning disabilities who sexually abuse. For example, the disinhibiting effect of alcohol was identified as contributing to the rape of a woman by a man with learning disabilities (Day, 1994). There was no evidence of drug use amongst the men in the research, and none of them drunk any more than an occasional alcoholic drink under the supervision of staff.

Understanding, knowledge and learning from experience

It is often suggested that men with learning disabilities who sexually abuse do not understand that their behaviour is unwanted or harmful to others (Murrey, Briggs & Davis, 1992; Verberne, 1990; Hingsburger, 1987) so, for example, there was a greater tolerance of Mr A's public masturbation than Mr D's because of the different expectations of their understanding of the social conventions of privacy.

A strategy which often flows from this is to assume that a man needs sex education because he has inadvertently made a mistake or misinterpreted social rules and conventions. This picture did not fit any of the men in this study and may provide a convenient, rather than an accurate, diagnosis.

Knowing something is 'wrong' can mean very different things. It might convey the notion of internalised standards in which empathy allows someone to anticipate harm to another person as a result of their actions and this is enough to stop them acting in certain ways. Alternatively it might be more of a calculation about possible consequences for oneself. People with learning disabilities are often not helped to develop an autonomous moral code in which they learn to judge what is right and wrong on the basis of how others are affected. 'Wrong' for them has been shown to equate with the disapproval of authority figures (Flynn, Whelan & Speake, 1985) and of the consequences of this for them (Heyman & Huckle, 1995). Using this perspective it is reasonable to say that Mr A knew his public masturbation was 'wrong' in the sense that he was able to anticipate the response he would get from staff which would be to tell him to stop or go elsewhere. The problem for him is not a **lack of knowledge** but rather his **accurate perception** that not much will happen.

A number of studies support this challenge to the notion that abusive behaviour comes from a lack of relevant knowledge and anticipation. One study involved a group of men with mild learning disabilities who had perpetrated a range of sexual assaults (Charman & Clare, 1992). These men were given a range of tests of sexual knowledge. While some gaps in the men's knowledge were found, overall their information was very good. Furthermore, none of the men had a problem in identifying the specific sexual crimes they had committed as unacceptable. Clear assessment needs to identify if any gaps in the men's knowledge are about sex, its significance, consent, appropriate partners, potential harm to others, social rules and conventions, or possible consequences. Clarity will remove the excuse from the man (that he abused because he did not know what he was doing) and from the service (that they need not act in response to his behaviour).

This does not however mean that these and other men appreciate the seriousness of their offences. A number of authors have been critical of the inconsistent responses men with learning disabilities receive for their abusive sexual behaviour (Hames, 1987), and the overall picture is of weak consequences to even serious sexual crimes (Thompson, 1997b). This is particularly the case when the victims are either other people with learning disabilities or women staff members. For example, Mr D's masturbation in front of female staff who are helping him with intimate care would receive a very different reaction if it was directed against women in the general public. Therefore, the problem may not lie in the men's misunderstanding of the consequences of their behaviour but rather that they know only too well that minimal, if any, sanctions will ensue.

The response to Mr B's assault on a child was typical of how agencies minimise the sexual behaviour of men with learning disabilities and in effect **define** it as not serious **for the man himself** thereby actively allowing him to continue the behaviour unchecked. We should then not be surprised that Mr B has a perception that what he did was not serious.

activity 2b   Mr B

Mr B

Mr B lived with his mother until he was found in their flat one day with her dead body – the flat was in a disgusting condition with faeces spread all around the rooms. He had not had contact with services before then and neighbours at this time reported that he used to roam markets with his mother collecting food discarded by vendors. At that point he entered learning disability services and was moved to a local hostel. This was ten years ago when he weighed just forty-five kilograms (seven stones). At the hostel they had several problems with his sexual behaviour, including him stripping naked by a window, gesturing masturbation to the neighbours, smearing faeces and urinating in public. The most serious incident occurred shortly after he arrived at the hostel when he started to take his penis out in public and thrust himself against a girl of 12 who was passing. For a while after this incident it was decided that Mr B should not go out unaccompanied. This arrangement had lapsed by the time he moved to a nearby group home when the hostel closed three years ago. He has been diagnosed by a psychiatrist as having hypomania and two years ago spent a short period in a psychiatric hospital which he did not enjoy. His physical condition is very much improved and he is no longer underweight.

The group home attempted to make links with his family and found his brother who showed no interest in re-establishing a relationship. Mr B had a couple of good friends at the hostel but they moved to other areas when it was closed down and he has not had any contact with them since that time. Otherwise the only people he names as important to him are the current staff of the group home. He still thinks a lot about his mother and the neighbourhood in which they used to live together.

In a case conference which followed the assault, Mr B asked if he would still be able to go on a scheduled social outing the following week.

What would your response be?

One strategy to help men with learning disabilities understand the seriousness of sexually abusing is for services to ensure that it consistently leads to serious consequences. A 'natural' consequence, unmediated by Mr B's service's desire to protect the man, would be for him to be brought into contact with the criminal justice system which may ultimately lead to prosecution and conviction. The legal system is greatly lacking in its accessibility to people with learning disabilities (ARC/NAPSAC, 1997) – both as potential perpetrators and victims of crimes. In effect this can be very undermining of services who are committed to ensuring justice for victims and an adequate reflection of the seriousness of abuse for perpetrators. We will look at how to maximise the impact of the legal system in **Part Three** but at this point offer the following example of how difficult this can be.

Dan

Dan, a man with Down's Syndrome, had been accused of raping a young woman with learning disabilities. The service was confident that something had taken place and contacted the local police. They arrived an hour later and drove Dan to the police station to be interviewed. On the way they stopped at McDonalds to buy him a hamburger, then introduced him to everyone at the station, and let him play with the dog there. No charges were ever placed and subsequently Dan was very happy seeing police officers when he was out.

In many ways the police fail to take crimes committed by (as well as against) men with learning disabilities seriously and this compounds the inconsistency of the service response. In one service a man with learning disabilities had forcibly had sex with a woman co-resident and we urged the service to convey how serious this was to the man concerned. They were resistant, arguing that it was not the **philosophy** of their service to apply sanctions – they wanted to limit the response to counselling for the man. Two months later another woman in the service was abused by the same man, and the service was still unwilling to do anything other than talk to him.

Masturbation, sexual fantasies and use of pornography

Above we saw how Down's Syndrome and Prader-Willi have an effect on masturbation but probably the most common cause of masturbation difficulties for men with learning disabilities is the side effect of prescribed medication. There are a wide range of drugs which are known to cause problems with erection and ejaculation. These include psychotropic drugs (for example, thioridazine, chlorpromazine and haloperidol [Sullivan & Lukoff, 1990]) and anti-convulsant drugs (for example, epilim). It is also possible that medication specifically given as a sexual suppressant may actually compound sexual problems because of the erectile dysfunction they cause.

If you are concerned that a man you are working with may have problems in this respect it is useful to check in a drugs guide like MIMS. It is also worth checking with the man himself if he notices any difficulties. It may be that the men do not understand why they are currently unable to masturbate when they could do it previously. There may be other reasons why this change has happened aside from medication, for example, stress or a punitive response from staff.

The following extract is taken from a conversation with Mr B. The exchange took place during the 16th meeting with the researcher, and was the first time Mr B had spoken so explicitly about masturbation. He had originally been prescribed thioridazine because of his unacceptable sexual behaviour. Thioridazine is known to cause problems with erection and/or ejaculation in between 30% and 60% of cases. No one had told Mr B this. The conversation started with Mr B talking about what sounded like a consented sexual contact with another man who used to live in the hostel with him.

Mr B:	[He] started pulling himself in the sink.
David:	What do you call that pulling himself?
Mr B:	Wanking.
David:	Yes, wanking himself off. And you saw him do it?
Mr B:	Yes.
David:	Are toilets a good place to do it?
Mr B:	Yes.
David:	Less chance of staff coming in.
Mr B:	Yes.
David:	Did they get cross when they found you?
Mr B:	Yes.
David:	Who did they tell off the most – you or Liam?
Mr B:	Liam. Done it many times he did in the sink. Used to clear it up after.
David:	Did you rub yours too?
Mr B:	No.
David:	Why not?
Mr B:	No, didn't want to.
David:	Have you ever?

Mr B:	Yes, I used to.
David:	You used to but not any more? Why not?
Mr B:	Can't get the feeling.
David:	Oh right. Do you know why that is?
Mr B:	I used it out.

If men do not have a problem with masturbation they are usually able to describe the different stages, once trust has been established (note it was not until the 16th meeting that Mr B felt able to talk so explicitly about masturbation). A typical conversation with such a man would be as follows:

Worker:	(*showing a line drawing of a man masturbating*) What's this man doing?
Man:	Playing with it.
Worker:	Yes, it's a good thing to do. Where's a good place to do it?
Man:	Bedroom.
Worker:	Yes, do you do it?
Man:	(*hesitant agreement by nodding*)
Worker:	Good, most men do it; it's a good thing to do. What happens when you play with it?
Man:	Gets hard.
Worker:	What happens if you keep rubbing it?
Man:	Gets hard.
Worker:	Yes, and what happens at the end?
Man:	White stuff comes out.

For some men it may be too confronting to talk about what they do, and it is easier to talk about what other men do. The worker is then left to consider whether the man's description of other men's masturbation is based on his own similar experiences or merely on observation.

It would be wrong to think that barriers to masturbation were helpful in stopping or reducing sexually abusive behaviour, or that the behaviour may be worse if there were no symptoms of sexual dysfunction. It may be that the abusive behaviour is in part motivated by the man's sexual inadequacy as was believed to be the case with Mr E.

Sometimes the unacceptable sexual behaviour of men with learning disabilities is identified as a direct outcome of 'sexual frustration'. With more able men, staff acknowledge the apparent lack of sexual opportunity – we will explore this more fully later (see pages 88–9). In the case of less able men, staff are typically identifying problems in masturbation as a major factor, which should lead them to ask:

- what evidence there is that the man is experiencing problems with masturbation?

- if it is possible that the man is masturbating unproblematically and appropriately in private?

- if there is evidence that the man has difficulties masturbating, how exactly is this contributing to his unacceptable sexual behaviour?

activity 2c   Problems with masturbation

Consider the scenarios below and try to decide how relevant the problems with masturbation are to the men's unacceptable and abusive sexual behaviours.

Mark

Mark has been taking medication for his epilepsy for a number of years. Staff who work with him report that they have never seen him with an erection or trying to play with his penis in any way. They are experiencing major difficulties when women staff are involved in his intimate care: he attempts to grab their breasts when they are helping him. These assaults often cause both pain and embarrassment to the women concerned.

Lloyd

Lloyd spends a lot of time masturbating, both in public and private but no one knows if he ever reaches orgasm. Sometimes when he tries to masturbate he becomes increasingly agitated and reacts quite violently when staff try to intervene to stop him doing it in public or to lead him somewhere more appropriate. Staff have been recording his episodes of violence for some time and have found that the vast majority of them occur when he is interrupted in the course of masturbating.

Matt

Matt has Down's Syndrome and though his parents know he plays with his penis, they have never seen any sign of ejaculation. There is no record of there being a problem with him exposing himself or trying to masturbate in public but at the day centre he regularly goes up to people, especially staff and less able people, and rubs his groin against them. This is assumed to be a sexually motivated act.

Of the three men in **Activity 2c**, Lloyd is the only one whose difficulties with masturbation are likely to be directly linked to his unacceptable behaviour. The records staff made are helpful in trying to confirm this because they discriminate between his general reaction to staff's expectations and his response to being interrupted while masturbating.

On occasion services may be required to help a man with learning disabilities who is having difficulties with the practicalities of masturbation or to intervene where a man's own technique risks injury to himself. Before doing any teaching they would be required to check that the problems are neither organic or caused by medication (see page 65). Any such teaching would have to be formally discussed and agreed. If it involved any actions which could be perceived as sexual touch, this could be interpreted as an offence under the *Sexual Offences Act* so a court decision might be needed before such a programme were instituted. There is little evidence to suggest that medication to reduce sexual drive would be helpful where there are problems with masturbation (see pages 120–122 for a discussion about sexual suppressant medication).

Fantasies can play a part in sexually abusive behaviour. Concern runs high, especially when men are known to fantasise about children or when non-consensual violence is involved. There is ample pornography available to confirm that both of these fantasies are commonplace across a spectrum of men with and without learning disabilities. What is not clear is how many men entertain these fantasies and how many actively seek opportunities to realise them.

Where abusive behaviour is linked to a man's fantasies, the acts are believed to be both a consequence, and a reinforcer of the fantasies. For example, if a man desires having sex with children and then acts this out, it subsequently provides additional images to add to his repertoire of fantasies. If he masturbates to his fantasies, this reinforces the link in his mind between sexual arousal, orgasm and partners who are too young or non-consenting, in turn making it more likely that his private fantasies will spill over into real abuse. This has been described as a 'cyclic' model of abuse (Wyre, 1990) when it is perpetrated by men without learning disabilities.

The extent to which fantasies play a part in the abusive behaviour of men with learning disabilities is more difficult to determine. Firstly there is some evidence that many men with learning disabilities do not fantasise – they do not hold distinct images in their minds of erotic scenarios. Instead, it may be the case that their sexuality is mainly experienced in the immediate here and now and in an exclusively physically way – the experience of touching and being touched (Swanson, & Garwick, 1990; Gebherd, 1973). The pleasure for some men with learning disabilities involved in sexual contacts with both women and men is often primarily linked to the physical sensation of penetration (anal or vaginal) and the gender of the person seems to be comparatively unimportant. One consequence of this is that where services are concerned about a man sexually abusing women, they should take seriously the risk of him also abusing men. One study showed that when men with learning disabilities abuse children or less able people with learning disabilities, both genders are equally vulnerable (Thompson, 1997b). It seems that vulnerability is more a factor in the men's choice of victim than gender.

The suggestion that men with learning disabilities might find it difficult to fantasise does make some sense because fantasies are essentially abstract thinking and cognitively quite complex. There is some agreement that it is difficult for men with learning disabilities to construct fantasies which are not based on actual events (Haaven, 1983) but clearly some men may engage in this type of thinking more easily than others. Often services will be very aware of service-users who use commercially available pornography as a stimulus for masturbation. We urge caution before you make simplistic assumptions about a man's fantasies, preferences (if any) and his abusive behaviour.

Mr B was one man whose sexually abusive behaviour may have been linked to fantasising and the use of quasi-pornography because of his collection of pictures of children. One question for staff was whether his assault of the girl was due to a specific sexual interest in children, or whether it could be explained more by her vulnerability. Clarification could help guide the nature of the care plan that is put in place to minimise the risk of further assaults.

Mr B's relatively innocuous collection of pictures ('*having been collected from TV magazines and other easily accessible publications*', see page 12) is no guarantee that he is not specifically sexually aroused by children. These are exactly the kinds of pictures men with learning disabilities *do* use to support fantasies of sex with children – they typically lack the cognitive skills to track down more definably pornographic images of children such as those found on the Internet.

However strong your concerns, you should be extremely cautious about identifying, or labelling a man as being specifically attracted to children. Such identification should only be made by a specialist in the field of sexuality, or a psychologist or psychiatrist. The caution is necessary to recognise the risks to the man if he is wrongly or prematurely identified as a paedophile. There is an understandable but also hyped-up public hostility to paedophiles at this time which can lead to an emotional response which displaces rational assumptions about risk and which compromises justice. Men with learning disabilities are particularly vulnerable if they are identified as sexually deviant as you can see from the examples in **Activity 2d**.

Because the consequences of sexual interest in children are so far reaching it is essential that services exercise caution and seek professional input into any such 'diagnosis'. Clearly it is difficult trying to identify someone's private inclinations, all the more so if they are not very articulate about sexual matters

activity 2d   Sexual interest in children

The following scenarios demonstrate what can happen when men with learning disabilities are identified as having a specific sexual interest in children.

Ronnie

Ronnie, a man with mild learning disabilities had invited a young boy of ten whom he met at the park into the flat where he lived by himself with minimal support. Once he was there he tried to have sex with the boy who resisted and then got away. The boy reported what had happened through his parents to the police. As a result, the man was detained temporarily under the Mental Health Act in a learning disability hospital. During this time an assessment revealed that he had a specific sexual interest in prepubescent boys. This single piece of information led to the man being moved to a more secure institution where he was to be held indefinitely. This move took place without even consulting the person who had made the assessment about what might be an appropriate service plan.

Greg

Greg was in his 60s and in addition to a mild learning disability, had increasing problems of mobility which meant that he was unable to walk more than a few metres without the support of workers. Whilst in transition from the institution where he had lived for many years to a staffed group home in the community, attention was focused on him talking about wanting young girls to be his girl-friends – these were children he saw in pictures or the staff's own children. An assessment showed that his interest in young girls was not a misunderstanding about appropriate ages for partners but that he was quite clear that he would like to touch them sexually – being particularly interested in their lack of pubic hair. Although there was no knowledge of Greg ever having sexually assaulted a child it was recommended that the group home should exercise some caution when children were around. However, the outcome of this discussion was that the place at the group home was withdrawn as a result of the staff's reaction to his sexual interest in children.

Do you think the outcomes of these situations were appropriate?

in the first place or if they have good reason to dissemble. One method used to establish men's actual (as opposed to reported) sexual fantasies is an instrument called a 'penile plethysmograph'. Basically (and it is basic), it measures changes to the size of a man's penis in response to a range of visual or auditory stimuli, in an attempt to establish what the man is aroused by. There are considerable ethical problems in the use of this instrument, not least with the necessity to expose men to abusive images to determine whether they are sexually aroused by them and the confusion about privacy which the assessment procedure entails. For this reason it is regarded as unethical to test boys in this way. We feel that for the same reasons it should not be used on men with learning disabilities.

Sensitive assessment may obviate the need for such a crude methodology. Although men with learning disabilities are less verbal than other men they are also less skilled at evading discovery or covering their tracks. They are also more likely to be naive and open in reporting their sexual interests which in itself creates ethical dilemmas. This does not mean that men with learning disabilities will necessarily answer direct questions about what their fantasies are, but they are usually less guarded about volunteering information. Here is a transcript of a recorded conversation with Mr B – the aim being to understand how he perceived children.

David: What's different about adults and children?

Mr B: Soft skin.

David: Who has soft skin?

Mr B: Little girls.

David: What else is special about little girls?

Mr B: No hair.

These were the first answers Mr B gave about differences between adults and children and required little prompting. Considering these responses alongside his collection of pictures of children and his previous assault on a child strongly suggests a specific sexual interest in children.

If a man with learning disabilities is believed to fantasise about children or anything else that is non-consensual, it is reasonable to want to stop him having these fantasies. Firstly the fantasy may be seen as a rehearsal of actual assaults but secondly the fantasies are seen as a way in to changing the behaviour itself. Two strategies have been tried:

■ substituting them with more 'normal' or 'acceptable' images, or

■ turning them into something unpleasant.

The first approach was used to attempt to change men's sexual interest in men when sex between men was still illegal and devalued and to substitute arousal to women. Despite the very severe and draconian methods used, including electric shock treatment, sexual orientation proved very resistant to change. From this it follows that encouraging men with learning disabilities who are sexually interested in children to use adult pornography will probably be ineffective in diminishing their desires towards children.

The second strategy to displace unacceptable fantasies has been to try to make them less appealing. A variety of techniques have been attempted with limited success. Although measuring improvements is very difficult, what is believed to be useful with men with learning disabilities is to help them to associate the abusive fantasies with images of what would happen to them if they turned their fantasies into actual assaults. In practice this has been done by trying to help the men associate a picture of a child with a picture of them experiencing the potential consequence of child abuse – for example, being put in prison.

Any attempt to influence or control abusive sexual fantasies should be directly supervised by a psychologist as it needs to take place in controlled surroundings and after exhaustive assessment. Token gestures like giving a man adult pornography depicting women should be resisted. **Part Three** makes alternative and more realistic suggestions about how sexual interest in children may be managed and contained.

You might also be worried about how a man's use of adult pornography may negatively influence his sexual behaviour. This was a concern in relation to Mr C who was known to have access to his brother's pornography. Although it was difficult to work out quite what this pornography depicted, it was clearly of men having sex with one or more women. In addition to this there were more general concerns that his brother's attitudes to women were unhelpful to Mr C and carried over into his behaviour around women staff and residents.

We saw in **Part One** that attitudes to pornography vary and there has been a long debate about whether pornography affects sexual behaviour. In the US, lobby groups have been campaigning to ban pornography depicting women on the grounds that it incites men to commit sexual crimes against women. Men who sexually abuse are believed to rehearse their sexual crimes by using pornography (Wyre, 1990). A contradictory view is that pornography can act as a means of controlling a man's sexual behaviour and a relatively harmless 'outlet'.

The situations in **Activity 2e** (page 79) represent the two opposing views about pornography identified earlier: while Martin's brother is concerned that the pornography is increasing the risk of abuse, the staff who worked with Chris believe that greater access to pornography may provide a partial solution to his problem behaviour. In both situations staff and carers have detailed knowledge about the men's use of pornography and power to control its use, which would not happen if the men were not in learning disability services. It is important to recognise, before making judgements, that we have little equivalent information about the extent of other men's use of pornography aside from the enormity of the pornography industry. Thus we need to be careful about describing either Martin's or Chris's behaviour as abnormal, or problematic.

Interestingly the staff's opinion of Chris's family's attitude to pornography was contradicted by Chris himself. In meetings with the researcher he said that he had previously bought magazines with his mother and they would be kept 'on top' in his bedroom. This made sense because his request to staff did not sound as if this was the first time he had tried to buy a magazine. This undermined the staff's opinion that his sexuality was being repressed and that this repression to some extent explained his abusive behaviour.

Martin's brother's concerns seemed to make greater sense – after all Martin was persistently talking about sex with staff at the day service in very crude and unwelcome ways. His use of pornography was also felt to be shaping his expectations of the sex he might have with any girlfriend, because he lacked the ability to separate the fantasy of pornography from the reality of relationships.

activity 2e   Harassing women staff

Consider the following two situations – in both cases the men were known to be sexually harassing women staff, including asking them to have sex with them and on occasion trying to grab at their breasts.

Martin

Martin's brother reported that he was worried about Martin's use of pornography. At home Martin spent a lot of time in his room looking at pornography showing women. This could be magazines or videos but recently he was almost continually viewing the pornography station on cable television. His brother had asked the social worker's advice as to whether he should limit Martin's use in any way, in particular to stop the subscription to the cable station. Staff agreed that this would be a useful start.

Chris

When out with a male member of staff from the day service, Chris indicated that he wanted to buy a Playboy style magazine from a newsagent. The staff member accepted this but was concerned about the reaction of his mother if Chris brought it home. Because of this it was suggested to Chris that it was kept safe in the office but that he could ask for it while at the centre to take it somewhere private. The staff's view was that Chris's sexuality was being unfairly denied by his family, and that this was part of the problem in his current abusive behaviour towards women staff.

Do you agree with the staff's suggestions in these cases?

Cultural factors

Turning away from the experiences and attributes of individual men, there are a number of cultural factors which coalesce to condone men's abusive behaviour.

'Culture' takes many shapes and sizes. It could be the philosophy of a group home, a world religion, or the social attitudes towards women and men in a community or country.

Most perpetrators of sexual abuse are men whether or not they have learning disabilities and because this is such a key issue it is unhelpful to hide behind gender neutral language and talk indiscriminately about 'people' with learning disabilities who sexually abuse.

Theorists bring their own perspectives to bear on why this should be so, with two models being put forward:

- one possibility is that there may be a biological predisposition for men to sexually abuse

- alternatively, societies may teach men behaviours and values which are consistent with sexually abusing.

The relative importance of these two factors is not clear. Feminists have focused largely on the second of these: **male socialisation**. They have highlighted that numerous institutions in society legitimise male power over women or over less powerful men, including marriage, the legal system, religions, hierarchies at work, sport, the medical profession. These and other more specifically sexualised structures reinforce ideas that women and to a lesser extent children are available for men's sexual gratification (for example, pornography and the fashion industry).

Work has shown that male power ('patriarchy') permeates learning disability services in many ways (Brown, 1989). One of the most clear is the predominance of women in direct support roles which reinforces the notion that women's role is to look after other people, while men are still disproportionately represented in management and 'hands off' positions. This has an impact on the readiness of services to address sexual harassment and abuse. However, it also fundamentally affects the social environment within which people with learning disabilities learn about relationships and behaviour. Although in many ways children and adults with learning disabilities have atypical life experiences, these are still commonly rooted in, and distorted by, patriarchal values. It has been suggested that men who feel less powerful than other men may take it out on women staff and service-users (Thompson, Clare & Brown, 1997).

Social attitudes also widely condone, or turn a blind eye to, certain types of sexual violence. Awareness of sexual abuse of children and of the prevalence and seriousness of domestic violence is still a relatively recent phenomenon. Initially it was women who spoke up about what had happened to them, and this has made it easier for other groups, including people with learning disabilities (Brown & Craft, 1989) and men, to speak out about their experiences of victimisation. It is important to recognise that although there is growing public condemnation of sexual abuse, social institutions such as the law are still lagging behind in their attitudes and practice. There have been recent changes, for example, in the way children are allowed to give evidence in court, but the treatment of victims of abuse who are brave enough to seek justice from the courts does little to suggest that the legal system has progressed far enough to fulfil its commitment to eradicating abuse.

The problems of justice are magnified further when the victim and/or perpetrator has learning disabilities. The criminal justice system often fails to engage with them so that, effectively, society is inadvertently letting these men off the hook when it comes to their crimes[1]. However, the men are also often excluded from community-based programmes which may help them to change or control their behaviour – they are discriminated against by being seen as unworthy of the most progressive treatments. Learning disability services often collude with (or at least fail to find a way of challenging) this double standard, because they rarely involve the police particularly when the men's victims also have learning disabilities (McCarthy & Thompson, 1997, and Brown & Stein, 1997). Abuse is also endemic in larger institutions, and yet these are often posited as part of the solution in cases where men with learning disabilities have abusive behaviours, instead of as part of the problem (Crossmaker, 1991, and McCarthy & Thompson, 1997).

Personal and family relationships

It is generally accepted that men's abusive behaviour can be linked to their life experiences, particularly those during childhood. With this in mind it is worth speculating about the emotional impact of the early lives of Mr A, Mr D and another man, Brian, whom we met during the course of this study.

Mr A

There have been at least two points in Mr A's life when everything and everyone around him changed. At the age of seven he was moved from the city to a residential school in the countryside. Then, when he was 20, he returned to the city to live in a newly established group home because the school was closing down. He has no contact with any family or anyone else who knew him before the group home. He is now 23 and is regarded as having no friends. Being black in an essentially white rural area is likely to have increased his sense of alienation.

---

[1] See the *Youth Justice and Criminal Evidence Act 1999*

Mr D

Mr D's mother left him in hospital shortly after she gave birth because she felt unable to cope with him. He was taken from the hospital to a local children's home. He stayed there until he was 12 when his behaviour was considered too difficult to manage. He then lived in a large hospital-style institution until it closed when he was 27. Since then he has been at a group home. The only contact he has from his time before leaving the hospital are Christmas and birthday cards from the house parents who looked after him all the time he was in the children's home.

Brian

Brian spent most of his childhood living in a children's home because his mother felt unable to manage him at home. There was no contact with the father. His mother, having come from another country just before he was born, was herself very isolated. Contact with the mother remained strong and she had him stay with her at home regularly. These visits continued after he moved into a group home at the age of 19 but then came to an abrupt end because of some violent behaviour he directed at her when they were alone. After this contact was maintained by her visiting the group home though this did not happen very frequently. A couple of years after his time at his mother's was suspended he became very upset. Eventually staff worked out that he was longing to spend time with his mother at her house. This was made possible by ensuring a staff member remained with him.

Unfortunately, these stories are not unusual amongst people with learning disabilities; it is remarkable that many people can somehow survive such experiences. Interestingly it was the least able men in the study who had to cope with the most traumatic changes identified above.

Marshall, who is one of the world's leading experts in working with men who sexually abuse, is clear that difficult experiences in childhood are a root cause of the kinds of loneliness which lead to abusive sexual behaviour. He sees abusing as an expression of the resulting emotional isolation:

> '...poor quality childhood attachments are understood to lead to a sense of alienation as an adolescent and adult, and this loneliness is a critical factor in the initiation and continuation of sexual offending'
>
> (Marshall, 1993)

For many people with learning disabilities emotional isolation is common at some stages of their lives. This may be partly because some people with learning disabilities have their own difficulties in developing and maintaining emotional relationships, but these are exacerbated by the way people around them respond to them whether at home, in school or in their neighbourhoods.

The presence of a child with learning disabilities can put enormous strains on family relationships, so that family **breakdown**, **violence** and **abuse** may be more common. It is also more likely that children with learning disabilities will be separated from their families at an earlier age than other children. Some, like Mr A and Mr D, may move into care in infancy with no further contact with their families. Alternatively, they may be sent for periods to residential schools or respite services. This is not to say that services do not attempt to foster relationships and emotional growth, but it is particularly difficult to provide continuity in these settings, particularly in the long term.

Relationships or 'attachments' within the family over time are also seen as crucially important in understanding why some men grow up to sexually abuse (Marshall, Laws & Barbaree, 1990). For example, amongst men who abuse, high rates of divorce and separation of their parents as well as violence between parents and towards children have been found (Faban & Wexler, 1988). But again, this is likely to be a contributing factor woven in with other complications. We know that many men who have lived through these same experiences do not end up as abusers. This was the case in one small study of men with learning disabilities (Gilby *et al*, 1989) where experiences of family breakdown and violence in childhood were found to be common histories regardless of whether the men had been identified as abusers or not.

Prior abuse

In our research, of six men who stayed in their family homes through childhood, two were known to have experienced extreme forms of physical violence at home. Both of these involved assaults by a male partner of their mother or female carer. Even though both these men turned up at learning disability services with physical signs of their abuse, there was no knowledge of police or child protection proceedings ever having been instituted. Nor were there records available to identify whether Mr A or Mr D had been physically abused during their time in institutions as children. Acknowledging prior abuse of the men is not an alternative to addressing their current abusive behaviour but it does seem to be a pervasive backdrop to any therapeutic interventions.

Sexual abuse may be cited specifically as a reason for the men's own sexual abusing. Amongst convicted male sex offenders rates of prior sexual abuse have ranged between 3% and 30% (Watkins & Bentovin, 1992). Even allowing for the difficulty which men experience in reporting their own victimisation, it is probable that prior sexual abuse affects only a minority of men who sexually abuse others. Having said this we do know that prior abuse is 'an important contributory, but not a necessary factor in the development of a perpetrator' (Watkins & Bentovin, 1992, p221). A number of studies have tried to provide a more detailed account of the nature of the link – any of the following increase the likelihood of a victim becoming a perpetrator:

- if he was abused by a man, or close relatives or multiple perpetrators

- if the abuse started at an early age or was sustained over a long period of time; and finally

- if the abuse was physically severe.

(Finkelhor, 1986)

These factors cumulatively affect the emotional damage of sexual abuse and its subsequent impact in terms of abusing behaviour.

When prior sexual abuse is looked at specifically in relation to men with learning disabilities who are sexually abusing, a number of studies shed light on how common the experience of sexual abuse is for all men and women with learning disabilities (Brown, Turk & Stein, 1995; McCarthy & Thompson, 1997). This means that a lot of men with learning disabilities will have been sexually abused, regardless of whether or not they go on to abuse others. Amongst abusers the rate of prior sexual abuse has been found to be close to 100% by some researchers (Corbett, 1996). However, one study found that none of a group of men with learning disabilities who had sexually abused children had themselves been abused (Gilby *et al*, 1989). Our own studies have emphasised the need to be cautious about simplistically attributing the behaviour of men with learning disabilities to their own abuse. Looking at a group of over 100 men with learning disabilities, over half of whom had perpetrated some form of sexual abuse, overall 23% had been previously sexually abused. If prior abuse was a major factor in predicting abusive behaviour we would have expected the highest rate amongst the abusers but this was not the case (Thompson, 1997). So the picture is similar to that of sexual abusers generally – most men with learning disabilities who abuse are unlikely to have been sexually abused themselves, and even for those where this has happened we need to be cautious about suggesting a direct connection. Moreover, when men with or without learning disabilities are sexually abused and receive timely support there is no inevitability about them going on to abuse others; they may be able to acknowledge the harm such abuse did to them and deal with their feelings appropriately and safely.

We are not denying that a connection exists for some men. We have both worked with men where the emotional connections between what has happened to them and what they are doing are manifest. What we are concerned about are people being too eager to find evidence of men having been abused, and then to blame their behaviour on this without questioning the validity of the link. It is almost as if they want the man to have been abused – instead of being critical of his abusive behaviour they can divert to feeling sorry for him.

Current relationships, social networks and service settings

We have seen that these men struggle with feelings of 'different-ness', that they may not understand or learn from the inconsistent messages they receive about their sexual behaviour, that they are exposed (as all men are) to pornography and to structural apathy in the face of abuse. We also saw that many had lived through traumatic childhoods and had disrupted relationships with families and carers. Perhaps it is no wonder that many of the men have arrived at a point in their lives where they experience intense loneliness and emotional isolation. This was the most striking common factor between the men in the study.

One way of documenting this is to draw the men's networks – the people they come into contact with and their relationships with them. There are different ways of doing this (Atkinson & Williams, 1990). For comparison you may want to draw your own network, either in a table as we have, or in a series of concentric circles which have the people you live and spend most time with in the middle and which work outwards to the people who are paid to be in your life like your doctor or dentist.

See Case checklist D: Networks

Mr B

Mr B says he does not have any friends. He talks about two friends, though, who used to live in the same hostel as him, but he has not seen or heard of them since the hostel closed two years ago when they moved to a different group home.

NETWORK

Family	Peers	Friends	Paid carers
Brother – one contact in over two years.	James lives in same home but there is minimal social contact between the two. Other service-users at day centre but none identified as friends nor contact outside of the service setting.	Two men who lived in the same hostel – no contact since they moved to another area when it closed two years ago.	Nine permanent staff at group home, common use of agency staff. Some particular favourites including one woman who has recently left. Staff at the day centre he attends.

Frank

Frank was another man we had contact with who had an even more sparse social network.

NETWORK

Family	Peers	Friends	Paid carers
Brother who he lives with, and extended family. Involvement is mainly 'looking after' him. He is commonly excluded from family gatherings because he is regarded as 'difficult'.	People with learning disabilities at the day centre, but he regards himself as more able than them and has very little to do with them.	None.	Five staff at day service, particularly the female manager from whom he gains a lot of practical and emotional support.

As you can see when you set it out in this way, both Mr B's and Frank's contacts are dominated by paid and unpaid carers. Frank refers to the staff at the day service as his friends and to the manager as his girlfriend, but this is not how the staff would describe these relationships and they are mindful that they are paid to provide a service to Frank. Mr B seems to have a better understanding of the difference between staff and friends, and when he says he does not have any friends he is, unfortunately, painting an accurate picture of his social network. Frank does have a great deal of contact with his family, in particular through his brother who took over the role of providing practical support at home after their mother died. However, the brother tends to exclude Frank from his own social network, and would not invite him out to the pub in the evening when he goes out to meet his own friends. Frank's wider family also provide him with some support, but this appears to be to help his brother out, more than to offer extended social opportunities to Frank. Mr B's contact with his family ended abruptly after his mother died, and it was only after a brother was traced through the Salvation Army that any contact was resumed. This led to one visit from his brother, and though he is keen to see more of him, Mr B has not heard from him in over a year, and the staff are reluctant to press him to stay in touch.

In many ways Mr B's and Frank's social networks are similar. Although they have a lot of contact with workers and other carers, as well as with other service-users, they do not have people in their lives that they can regard as friends. For Mr B this means that he spends a lot of time at home sitting alone in the lounge. Frank also spends a lot of time at home alone, but also goes out alone and roams around the local area by himself. Mr B was acutely aware of the absence of friends in his life and remembered the two male friends he used to live with at the old hostel – friendships that ended because the hostel was closed down. Mr B does not complain about this or show much enthusiasm to develop new friends, he has become resigned to the current situation.

Frank's abusive behaviour involved sexually harassing women working on market stalls, but also a couple of incidents of indecent exposure to teenage girls. Appreciating his emotional isolation was significant in understanding and responding to his behaviour and two things confirmed this view:

■ Frank consistently spoke of his longing for sex and a girlfriend which workers interpreted as his belief that this was the only way his isolation could be broken

■ After the sexual assaults in public had been reported, Frank received a day service for the first time, and since then there have been no further assaults, suggesting that the emotional support he received from staff was instrumental in helping him to avoid further abusing. His demands on staff since then have been related to how stressed he is in other parts of his life.

Unfortunately Mr B's and Frank's social networks are not unusual. There are many men (and women) with learning disabilities who spend too much time by themselves, either at home or wandering around the neighbourhood. Some may seem resigned, as Mr B does, while others acknowledge it as unbearable. Isolation on this scale may lead to a range of difficult behaviours whose underlying origins are either cries for attention or misguided attempts to get company including:

- self-injury
- arson (Murphy & Clare, 1991)
- seeking sex with men in public toilets (Thompson, 1994a)
- sexual assaults.

Tony

Tony was another man we met. He lived in a bedsit and appeared to have no friends, his family limited the contact he had with them. Without any day service he was extremely isolated and was very unhappy with his situation. He wanted it to change and believed that getting married and having children, like his brother, would be a solution and that all he needed to do was find a girlfriend. However, where was he to find someone? What he did was to try talking to women on buses who got very nervous about his intentions. They would try to get away from him, and he would then try to hold on to them. These scuffles were then defined as sexual assaults. Although in other circumstances it might have seemed naive to accept his account that the assaults were basically about him wanting to get a girlfriend, this did seem to be the case because they took place in broad daylight when there were other people around.

Staff have recognised isolation as a factor in difficult sexual behaviours but often they reduce this to the notion that the men sexually abuse because their opportunities for consenting sexual relationships are so restricted (Hingsburger, Griffiths & Quinsey, 1991). Often they are implicitly talking about how difficult it is for the men to have sex with women (Haaven, 1983; Hames, 1987). What is less often considered are the opportunities which exist, and are taken up, for the men to have sex with men (Cambridge, 1997). Men with learning disabilities often have more opportunities to have sex with men in both institutional and community settings but these sexual contacts are usually unsupported by, and as a result are hidden from, staff. The men fear the response of staff and this makes what are potentially high risk activities such as meeting men for sex in public toilets, even less safe (Thompson, 1994a).

Mr E

Mr E's harassment of women staff was understood by some staff to be linked to 'sexual frustration'. Staff drew attention to his inability to masturbate and both a lack of knowledge and experience of sex with other people as reasons for this frustration. However, his lack of experience of sex was contradicted when he told one of us that over a period of time he had had sex with another man who attended his day service.

It is not uncommon for staff to underestimate the sexual knowledge and experience of men with learning disabilities who sexually abuse. The assumption that the men have no 'outlets' for sex may be a way of avoiding the uncomfortable truth that they are motivated to sexually abuse **in addition to having**, rather than because **they cannot find**, other sexual partners.

The idea that abuse is the result of restricted sexual opportunities has also been widely discredited in the mainstream literature on perpetrators without learning disabilities. Our difficulty with it, apart from its inaccuracy, is that it gives rise to the suggestion that a valid direction for 'treatment' is to help the man get a girlfriend. There are a number of problems with this. The heterosexist assumption about the man's sexuality is one, but more pressing is the risk of exploitation to women who are held out as potential partners, when the man has already proved himself to have little regard for the rights and feelings of others (Clare, 1993). Seemingly unaware of these risks, many workers proceed with programmes for men with learning disabilities which are about helping them to get a partner – working to ensure men know how to have sex with women, and acquire 'dating' skills. All men with learning disabilities need good sex education and social skills training, teaching them about respectful sex with both men and women, irrespective of whether they have sexually abused.

A further feature of service settings is the ease with which men with learning disabilities have access to vulnerable victims. The literature about men who sexually abuse children differentiates between those who have easy access to children through their families or jobs and those who put resources into manipulating their contacts, targeting and grooming potentially vulnerable children (Waterhouse, Dobash & Carnie, 1994). From this work it is clear that access to victims affects rates of abusing. Other men may travel to the far east to exploit child prostitutes in poor countries (Kelly *et al*, 1995), or buy sex at home or through the internet. Men with learning disabilities are unlikely to have either the knowledge, skill or finance to exploit these avenues. However, although men with learning disabilities have less control than other men over the people they befriend or live with, they are often placed in settings where access to vulnerable people is almost unlimited.

See Case checklist E: Identifying factors

part two

Putting It All Together –
Models of Abuse

W e have seen that no single factor is adequate in
explaining the sexually abusive behaviour of men.
Their past and present personal lives interact with
their current service settings and personal isolation in
a culture which presents them with confusing images of sex and male
violence. Instead of addressing the risks in a fragmented way, workers
in the field have developed multi-layered models of abuse which try
to predict how the personal and external factors interact. One of the
most influential of these syntheses was developed by Finkelhor in
relation to child sexual abuse (Finkelhor, 1984). He identified four
necessary conditions for a man to sexually abuse:

- motivation to sexually abuse

- overcoming internal inhibitors

- overcoming external inhibitors

- overcoming the resistance of the victim.

The motivation is the man's desire to have some kind of sexual contact
with a vulnerable or unconsenting partner. For men with learning
disabilities the motivation may be more simplistic – the desire for
sexual contact without an awareness of the social significance of this
behaviour.

Internal inhibitors are the controls a man might place on himself
to stop him acting out his desires. This may include conscience, guilt
or fear of reprisals. As we have said above, many men with learning
disabilities may have limited internal inhibitors because they find it
difficult to empathise with the feelings of other people, or they may
have had inconsistent responses to previous incidents of abuse and
therefore not appreciate the scale of the sanctions which could be
applied.

When a man is motivated to abuse, and has on some level justified the action to himself, he still needs to place himself in a position where he has access to vulnerable people – to overcome the external inhibitors. For child abusers this can mean hanging around schools, or developing relationships with mothers. Similarly for men who abuse adult women this may involve developing a relationship with the woman or stalking women in places where their safety is compromised. But as we have seen, men with learning disabilities do not have to put much effort into accessing victims – they abuse the child with whom they are left alone, the vulnerable people with learning disabilities who have no choice but to share residential or day services with them, or the women staff who are paid to provide intimate support to them.

According to this model, the final step for abuse to become a reality is for the abuser to overcome any resistance put up by the victim. When men with learning disabilities abuse other people with learning disabilities who may be frail, have limited communication skills or sensory impairments, there may not be any resistance – their vulnerability making them 'safe' victims. When they abuse women staff they may play on the ambiguity of the caring role and target women who are new or are perceived to have low status within the hierarchy.

Although there are other similar models of abusing behaviour we have found Finkelhor's framework valuable because of its simplicity and usefulness in helping to assess risk and draw up comprehensive care plans. On the pages which follow we have applied this framework to the five men we feature as case studies throughout this manual.

A theme which crops up again in the planning stage is the balance between expecting the man to put things right by changing his own motivation or internal controls and the extent to which the service has to put in place external controls and protection for vulnerable people. You will see that while it is very difficult to change motivation or to help the man develop the necessary cognitive processes which will allow him to control his own behaviour, you can attend to the external controls and to some extent strengthen the position of vulnerable people, particularly where the man abuses within services. By sharing the ideas in this manual with staff you can make sure that they know they can talk openly about any sexual behaviour they dislike, allowing them to report and challenge the man. You can also take steps to ensure that he is not placed alongside vulnerable service-users who do not have the strength or the skills to resist.

By using **Finkelhor's Model** to locate the past and present conditions which have led to the man's behaviour we hope you have laid the groundwork for effective planning around him and his service.

See Case checklist F: Finkelhor's model

FINKELHOR's MODEL FOR THE CASE STUDIES

	Motivation to abuse	Overcoming internal inhibitors	Overcoming external inhibitors	Overcoming the resistance of victims
Mr A	▪ Sexual feelings – though not abusive ▪ Sometimes bored	▪ Has a limited understanding of the importance of privacy ▪ Does not appreciate sanctions due to inconsistent and weak responses at times when he has previously masturbated publicly	▪ Indiscriminate about who he masturbates in front of. People always around except when he is alone in his bedroom or in the bathroom	▪ People witnessing the masturbation do not have an opportunity to avoid their exposure
Mr B	▪ Sexual feelings ▪ Sexual interest in children	▪ Low self-esteem – extreme social isolation a major contributory factor. ▪ Unconcerned about consequences for himself ▪ Difficulty empathising with victims ▪ Difficulty for him to understand that he could have any control over where or with whom he lives ▪ Mental health problems possibly exacerbate difficulties of self-control	▪ Hangs around schools to meet children	▪ Sudden attacks which the victims have little opportunity to avoid, but which they have the chance to escape from
Mr C	▪ Sexual feelings ▪ Limited knowledge of sensitivity in sexual relationships	▪ Conceals all sexual contacts because he feels staff would be negative ▪ Learning disability and limited sex education combine to give him an incorrect picture of the seriousness of his behaviour	▪ Victim shares same residential service	▪ Victim positive about the possibility of a relationship with him because of his high status within the service ▪ Dishonest promise that agreeing to sex would ensure a relationship ▪ Victim naive about the reality of the relationship having had limited support around personal relationships

FINKELHOR's MODEL FOR THE CASE STUDIES (continued)

	Motivation to abuse	Overcoming internal inhibitors	Overcoming external inhibitors	Overcoming the resistance of victims
Mr D	▪ Sexual feelings ▪ Reinforced by the responses of some women staff to his assaults	▪ Low self-esteem through broken attachments, limited social network, feeling different because of physical features of Marfan's Syndrome and having a learning disability ▪ Learning disability and lack of sex education both lead to limited awareness of the social significance of his behaviour	▪ Women not men staff employed in service ▪ Women staff required to attend to some aspects of his intimate care	▪ Uses 'surprise' so the women have no opportunity to prevent sudden assault
Mr E	▪ Sexual feelings ▪ Curiosity about other men's penises linked to his under-developed sexual organs	▪ Low self-esteem linked to feeling different because of Prader-Willi Syndrome ▪ Learning disability and limited sex education compound limited awareness of the significance of his behaviour	▪ Shares service with vulnerable people ▪ Limited staff supervision. Followed other man into the toilets	▪ No resistance because of vulnerability of the man

part
three

Service Planning

In this section we explore three aspects of the service's response to abusive and unacceptable sexual behaviour.

First of all we look at the issue of **responsibility** – at how much we can expect the men to take responsibility for their behaviour and who else must play a part. This involves a consideration of culpability, in other words of how much each man is 'to blame' for his behaviour and to what extent he can be expected and/or left to change or manage it. Once the issue of responsibility has been clarified we are ready to move on to key questions with regard to confidentiality – what information should be recorded and who should have access to it?

Secondly, we look at the range of possible **responses** which can be made to the men's behaviour, at how effective they are and at the practical and ethical issues they throw up – most significantly to the dilemmas of applying sanctions. We look at:

- responses which aim to change what the man does

- responses which seek to minimise the harm he does to others

- strategies for risk management and containment.

Thirdly, we look at the service system and the mechanisms which exist for co-ordinating the different inputs of day and residential services, employment and leisure, and specialist and professional expertise – this is what we have termed in the subtitle of this workbook the system's **response-ability**. Theories, as we said in **Part Two**, may help you to understand a man better and even to devise a way of working with him but this will come to nothing if:

■ these different parts of the system cannot work together

■ care plans are not drawn up and properly implemented, funded and evaluated

■ one hand does not know what the other is doing

■ the psychologist's advice about a particular programme is contradicted by residential workers

■ a man meets different responses in his day placement and at home.

Finally, we draw specific attention to the complex ethical issues arising when trying to formulate responses to men who abuse, and provide a set of questions by which to scrutinise your own work.

part three

1 Taking Responsibility

Underlying service and worker cultures

We saw in **Part Two** that the kinds of explanations you draw on shape the kinds of responses you seek to make. A service which thought sexual behaviour was primarily learned would seek to put educational or behavioural programmes in place and emphasise the need for consistent responses to the man's behaviour. On the other hand a service which located the problem in the present isolation of a man might look to build up his network and social relationships. We also challenged some myths and assumptions about what causes abusive sexual behaviour which may have *mis*informed your interventions in the past.

Accepting the challenge

Some of the theories, especially those which focus on the legacy of a difficult past or on the recycling of past harm into present abuse can have a fatalistic tone to them which discourages positive action and may even paralyse the service. If you think that there is nothing you *can* do about something almost certainly you *will* do nothing. Being sympathetic may lead you to minimise the behaviour and tolerate the harm it does to others rather than re-direct energy into trying to put things right in the current everyday lives of these men.

Is the service-user responsible?

One key issue which should determine your approach more than anything else is the extent to which you think the men *are* responsible and *can take* responsibility for their actions (see **Case checklist G: Degree of Responsibility**). This may, and we will argue should, vary for different men in line with the assessments you carried out in

Part One. These helped you to discriminate between deliberately targeted assaults and behaviours which had been misguided or misunderstood. However, you may base your judgements more on a blanket 'stance' than on careful consideration of individual cases and circumstances like the service we cited on page 70 which said that it was not their philosophy to impose sanctions for *any* service-user.

However, some of the men could be seen to be acting deliberately and autonomously, whereas for others there may be a range of mitigating circumstances in the man's past or present lives which lead you to assume that he was not responsible for his actions. If individual men with learning disabilities are seen as not wholly responsible for their actions then who is? Will your service take responsibility for managing his sexual behaviour in the same way as you would manage other risk-laden activities such as crossing the road, managing his money, seeking appropriate health care on his behalf and so on. If the service fails to take this responsibility there are significant risks to the man and to those whom he may abuse.

Making judgements

Staff make a judgement about how responsible individual service-users are for their actions based on their knowledge of the man, the nature of the sexual assault, the victim and their wider beliefs about sexual abuse.

The underlying assumptions which inform this judgement are fundamental to understanding how services respond to men with learning disabilities who sexually abuse. For example, if key people are strongly influenced by suggestions that the reasons for the abuse are beyond the men's control, they may be less inclined to advocate punitive measures. In many ways the legal system operates in this way with respect to any crime a person with learning disabilities may commit. Behind the notion of being 'unfit to plead', and the attempts to divert people with learning disabilities who are suspects away from both the courts and prison, is the idea that people with learning disabilities are not fully responsible for their actions.

You may want to review pages 32–33 where we set out a scheme for assessing the intention and seriousness of the behaviour and differentiated between **unacceptable** and **abusive** sexual behaviour. It follows that where a man with learning disabilities has no intention to sexually offend, he is less responsible for his actions than a man who deliberately did so. Other reasons why individual men may be partly 'excused' is where they have been abused themselves, where they do not understand the impact or seriousness of their actions, or where they are known to have had multiple stresses and a history of broken attachments. The validity of these as explanations and justifications were explored in **Part Two.**

Is the service responsible?

So far we have thought about whether the man should be held responsible but the second part of the question we asked is just as important. If he is not able to fully take responsibility, then who is going to? Services may be willing to excuse the man for his abusive behaviour but this is not always followed by a recognition of their own ensuing responsibility. This transfer of responsibility is a logical consequence of such an assessment given that services are implicitly charged with exactly those responsibilities that service-users cannot manage for themselves. Acknowledging that an individual man's abusive sexual behaviour is **to some extent** out of his control requires services to see themselves as partly responsible. Services (even properly sanctioned secure environments such as prison, special hospital or regional secure units) cannot completely rule out the possibility of an assault. However, based on their knowledge and assessment of a man's prior history, they must take all **reasonable** steps to prevent a man from abusing.

activity 3a   Service responsibility

Read the following case studies and think about how responsible Gregory, Noah, Nick and Malcolm are and what responsibility should have been taken by their respective services:

Gregory

Gregory has a history of sexually harassing both women with learning disabilities and women staff. Staff at his group home think that his social isolation might be a contributory factor. In response to this they make arrangements for him to attend a social club for people with learning disabilities. No one at the club is told about his history. On the second occasion he attends, two women with learning disabilities who are regular participants are absent. A phone enquiry reveals that they are avoiding Gregory because he had said some rude things to them the week before.

Noah

Within a large institution, Noah had gained a reputation for sexually exploiting less able people, who were often scared of what he might do if they tried to resist. Since he moved out of the hospital Noah has developed a relationship with a woman at the day centre. The staff who work with him are supportive of the relationship and are making arrangements for the two to have private time together. They have decided to keep his history confidential from the woman and her carers as they believe he should be given a fresh start now he is living in the community. One day his girlfriend complains that he forced her to have sex even though she was clear she did not want to.

continued...

Nick

Nick is a man with severe learning disabilities who needs help in the bathroom. On a number of occasions he had grabbed the breasts of women staff whilst they were supporting him with his intimate care. New staff are particularly vulnerable to these assaults. There are no similar problems when intimate care is provided by a man.

Malcolm

Malcolm, an unemployed man, had grabbed a woman's breast at a local shopping centre. The police who apprehended him did not believe it was serious enough to press charges but referred him to social services because they thought he may have some sort of learning disability. Although Malcolm had not had any previous contact with learning disability services and seemed to cope with the practicalities of life with a little support from his family, it was suggested that he attends a day service for people with learning disabilities and that he receives individual counselling from the psychologist attached to the unit. Shortly after his arrival at the service, he was found to have taken sexual advantage of a number of less able and unassertive women with learning disabilities who use the service.

■ Are the men fully responsible for these assaults?

■ Are there things the service should have done to prevent the abuse?

If a service fails to act appropriately where there is an **acknowledged** risk of abuse, it must take a share of the responsibility for acts of abuse which this negligence gives rise to. From the scenarios in **Activity 3a** it could be argued that it was negligent of the services to keep the abusive histories of both Gregory and Noah confidential as this put the women who were abused in unacceptably vulnerable positions. Similarly it is legitimate to suggest that the failure to insist on same-sex intimate care for Nick who had a history of assaulting women during this process makes the service responsible for the women's experiences and liable as employers for failing to ensure their safety.

We are arguing that services are responsible when they fail to act on information they have. However, where does this leave the social club which Gregory goes to? They had not been told about Gregory's history so could not take any special precautions. In this case the group home could be held to account for failing to pass on this information. This raises the critical issue of confidentiality which we address in the section below.

Confidentiality

This section looks at the management of information about men with learning disabilities who sexually abuse. It looks at what should be recorded and where, as well as in what circumstances this information should be passed on to, or discussed with, other individuals or agencies. We also consider what should happen if men with learning disabilities disclose further incidents of abuse or aspects of their sexual experiences which had previously been unknown.

The scenarios in **Activity 3b** illustrate the inconsistency of current practice with regard to the management of information. Decisions are made on the basis of a number of often conflicting principles and assumptions.

activity 3b   Information management

Liam
At an assessment meeting staff told the psychologist that, on a number of occasions, a staff member who had since left found Liam in a compromising position with other men at the day centre. Staff were very anxious that he received some form of sexual counselling to stop this. An examination of the case files could not clarify or confirm these incidents. Nor did it seem that any action had been taken against Liam or any support given to the other men.

Rob
Rob's behaviour with women staff was causing considerable concern. There were one or two whom he would not leave alone and if he did not get the attention he was seeking he would sometimes swear at them, using sexually explicit language. At a case conference, with Rob and his mother present, one woman who had been on the receiving end of this behaviour raised it for discussion. The chair of the meeting acknowledged that it was a problem but said it was too private to deal with in the meeting, and suggested that the two of them talked together afterwards.

Jeremy
Jeremy had been living in an institution for 20 years. He had been admitted initially because of a sexual assault against a child. Now that the hospital was closing, he was due to be resettled for the community. The resettlement team could not find any details of what the original sexual assault had been.

continued...

> **Richard**
>
> *Richard had been referred for sexual counselling after he had grabbed the breast of a woman at the day centre. During this work he said that he wanted to 'rape' this same woman. The counsellor did not report this statement to anyone in the service concerned but did discuss it with his external supervisor whose opinion was that 'it was good that Richard could express his aggression in the sessions'.*

■ Do you think knowledge about these men's sexual behaviour had been appropriately recorded and passed on in these examples?

Sex and privacy

One reason why services keep poor records about sexual as opposed to other forms of challenging behaviour is that sexual issues are considered to be particularly private. This makes some sense when talking about sexual expression where no one is victimised but it is unfounded in situations where people have been, or are at risk of being, exploited. There should be nothing private about sexual behaviour which unwilling people are forced to be a part of. So at Rob's meeting, if the expectation was that current needs were to be discussed, it would have been very appropriate to discuss his behaviour towards women staff. The chair's suggestion to meet privately could be seen as a way of minimising the seriousness of the behaviour. By suggesting that this was something which should be taken up privately by a member of staff who had been on the receiving end of it, the manager was colluding the myth that it could be seen as her problem rather than a problem for Rob and for the service – this kind of victim blaming is a wholly inappropriate stance for an employer to take.

The women with learning disabilities in the social club also paid the price for the decision taken by Gregory's service (see **Activity 3a**, page 99). Deciding what to pass on can be even more complicated when the issue is not only within a service but across agency boundaries, where there are often no formal agreements about what information should be shared. For example, we found one social services department which was unwilling to disclose the results of an investigation with a day centre, of an incident in which one service-user abused another within their shared residential home, even though they both attended the day service together. Increasingly adult protection policies are stipulating that information should be shared on a **need-to-know** basis and that prevention of abuse should take priority as it does in children's services.

Relatives are often kept in the dark because staff confuse rules about disclosure of sexual abuse with privacy in relation to consenting sexual behaviour. The latter might be withheld from parents if those concerned want it to be, but different norms should be applied if it is information about abusing or victimisation which is at issue. One reason for this is that families can be powerful advocates to ensure justice and also other appropriate responses. It also prevents accusations of abuse being 'swept under the carpet'. Of course there are exceptions and many policies will spell these out. Exceptions might include instances where someone is able to make their own decision about the help they want in the aftermath of abuse, or where they may judge that their parents will take actions which will go against their wishes – for example, by removing them from services or by restricting their movements (see *No Secrets*, Department of Health, 2000).

The presence of Rob's mother (see **Activity 3b**) at his case conference may have been why the chair avoided any discussion of his sexual harassment in this setting. However it might have been reasonable to have this discussion with her if she is still actively involved in Rob's support. What went wrong here was that the matter was brought up as last-minute business, with people unprepared. Given that these incidents had been happening over a considerable period of time, this aspect of Rob's behaviour should clearly have been on the agenda.

Choice

Although user choice is quite rightly a keystone of new service philosophies, this is sometimes cited as grounds to inhibit a useful flow of information between services. Where sexually abusive behaviour is an issue staff should make individual judgements. Some staff may question whether Rob's mother (see **Activity 3b**) should be at all involved in his care management since Rob is an adult, or query whether Ian's girlfriend should be told about his history. They may suggest that it is resolved by asking the men concerned and accepting their decision. However, there are contradictions here: staff are usually very supportive of the provisions in the criminal justice system which divert men with learning disabilities away from prisons – reflecting a view that men with learning disabilities who sexually abuse are not fully responsible for their actions – and yet they are willing to accept all the choices the men may take with regard to the management of their behaviour as if they had been fully responsible.

It is important to recognise that the victims of these men's behaviour **have not had a choice** about being sexually abused or harassed. It is, as we saw above, a service responsibility to effectively manage the men's behaviour. This does not mean that the men concerned should be excluded from debates about their management, rather that their voice should be seen as one amongst a number of stakeholders who include other service-users, staff and others responsible for designing appropriate service provision. The men's choice cannot be privileged as the last word when it is their behaviour which has caused offence.

Reporting

The professional role and occupational culture of different staff also influence what information is shared and recorded. Richard's counsellor (see **Activity 3b**), like many accredited therapists, abides by a strict code of confidentiality, but guidelines such as those issued by the British Association of Counselling also acknowledge exceptions such as risk of committing a crime (British Association for Counselling, 1990). It is important to note that in work with other sexual abusers such disclosures would always be acted upon and a client centred approach is regarded as inappropriate (Waterhouse, Dobash & Carnie, 1994). A bottom line for therapists around confidentiality should be the *Children Act 1989* and *No Secrets* (Department of Health, 2000) which insist that any risk to a child or vulnerable adult should be reported immediately to an appropriate statutory authority (health, social services or education) or to the NSPCC. Although the situation is less categorical when the person at risk is a vulnerable adult, local authorities have comparable interagency agreements which spell out the expectations on their behalf.

The passage of time

Noah's case study (see **Activity 3a**) illustrates that many people believe that men with learning disabilities who have sexually abused should be allowed to move on at some time, and not be clouded by their history. This can obviously help prevent prejudice against the men, however the loss of that history can also mean that unacceptable risks are taken unknowingly. Moving the man may say more about the service than the man, and reflect a desire to get rid of him rather than an accurate assessment that his behaviour no longer presents a risk. Generic work with sexual abusers tells us that single incidents are rare and that abusers often continue to abuse over many years. This information suggests that services should assume that the man **will continue to pose a risk unless there are clear indications otherwise**, rather than maintain an optimistic outlook without real grounds for doing so.

Guidance on recording

We saw on page 23 that concerns about the accuracy and fairness of recorded information often lead staff to err on the side of not putting anything on record. To minimise the risk of undue prejudice without jeopardising the benefits of retaining information for careful risk assessment and management, the following guidance is suggested for recording incidents of abuse:

■ Records should be as *specific* as possible – including the nature of the sexual abuse and the way the man managed to override the wishes of his victims. This information is crucial in profiling any cycle of offending behaviour. They should also include details of the immediate and longer term response made by the service and the eventual attitude of the man to the incident. These last details will help services to evaluate which, if any, previous responses have been effective. Full recording also allows for previous incidents to be examined under a fresh light as our understanding of sexual issues for people with learning disabilities evolves or as new information about this particular man comes to light (see **Case checklist C: Recording the behaviour**).

■ Information should be recorded *as soon as possible after the incident*, by the people closest to it. Ideally this would include the accounts of both the victim and the perpetrator.

If an investigation *fails to reach a conclusion about what took place, details should still be recorded*. This may be necessary even if a man with learning disabilities denies allegations and no clarification was possible as to what exactly took place. Over time, a picture may build up of a series of such allegations which may help to validate and understand future reports. There are certainly civil liberty issues at stake, but a failure to record appropriately detailed information may indirectly impact on the civil liberties of future victims.

Even where investigations are inconclusive, it can be very helpful to say what the outcome of the investigation was and to offer a view of what was believed to have taken place, with a note about the status of this information and the degree of confidence expressed within the investigating team that this is a reasonable account. This is particularly important when the potential victims are people with severe learning disabilities, who may have limited ways to describe what has happened to them. For example, if a woman with severe learning disabilities is found distressed in a room with her underwear dishevelled, just after a man is seen leaving the room, it could be very difficult to be sure what exactly did happen but it would seem very likely that the man had committed a sexual assault.

Men with learning disabilities and/or their advocates should, where realistic, be made aware of the records which have been made and be given an opportunity to register any disagreement they may have about what is held on their file.

On page 106 are examples of appropriate recording for some of the potentially abusive behaviour of the men in the case studies for you to use as a model for recording the behaviour of men with whom you may have contact.

INCIDENT REPORT CONCERNING MR B

Date...

Written by..

Position...

On the 5 January Mrs Smith came to the group home to complain that her daughter had been sexually assaulted by Mr B. She told the staff member on duty, and later confirmed the details with me the following day, about what she had observed in Manor Park at about 3pm that afternoon. Her eight-year-old daughter was playing some distance from her mother on her tricycle. Mr B had approached her daughter and seemed to try to talk to her, then moments later he was seen to have put his hand up the girl's dress. Her mother immediately shouted which led him to run in the opposite direction. She was able to identify Mr B with the help of another woman who said she regularly saw him in the park and had at times talked to him. When I talked to Mr B about this incident he appeared guilty and said he had been in the park and talked to the girl – he said he had asked her what her name was, but denied trying to touch her. We found out later that Mr B would visit the park almost daily when he went out to the local shops. The park is not en-route to the shops and is a further five minutes walk away from the shops.

INCIDENT REPORT CONCERNING MR C

Date...

Written by..

Position...

During a sex-education group conducted at the day service, Ingrid said that Mr C was 'doing it to her' and 'it hurt when he put it in'. On further discussion it appeared that she was letting him have sex with her because she was afraid that he would stop being her boyfriend if she refused. She said the sex took place late at night when he would come into her bedroom. There was no indication that Ingrid was enjoying the sex but she was positive about having Mr C as a boyfriend. Mr C was approached because we were afraid she was being exploited. He initially denied any relationship with Ingrid, instead talking about having a girlfriend at the day centre. On pressing him further he admitted to going into Ingrid's bedroom at night and having sex with her and justified this by saying he was not able to have sex with his girlfriend because her parents would not let her. We concluded that Mr C was exploiting Ingrid's vulnerability.

Guidance on sharing information

Once records are made about potentially sexually abusive behaviour of men with learning disabilities, decisions follow about where these records should be held and who, if anyone, has access to them. Our experience is that in services more problems result from information *not being shared* than from *being shared carelessly*. Furthermore, where services are unwilling to share information, nominally on the grounds of protecting the rights of service-users, they may also be operating to protect themselves; for example, not disclosing incidents of sexual abuse between service-users to either family members, inspectors, purchasers or the police, conveniently conceals any negligence on the part of the service. We believe that even the victim's unwillingness to report abuse should not be taken as an automatic veto, or sufficient grounds to ensure that people outside the service itself are not made aware of what has happened. The *National Minimum Standards for Care Homes for Adults* (Department of Health, 2003) requires notification of serious incidents affecting residents' welfare. Without this there can be no independent check on the continued safety of the victim, or the soundness of the service.

Where a man with learning disabilities is believed to have sexually abused we strongly recommend that the following guidelines regarding the holding and passing on of this information be followed. This holds true whether there is just one potential incident or a long history of proven assaults.

- The purchaser/commissioner should be made aware of this information and hold it indefinitely on file so that it is available whenever the man's services might change.

- The information should be made available to the management of any service through which the man is likely to come into contact with vulnerable people. By implication this includes any service which is accessed by other people with learning disabilities, such as any residential or day service for people with learning disabilities, leisure clubs, respite services, holiday placements, fostering or adult placement schemes. The information should be carefully shared with the provider as part of the process of negotiating the placement.

- Staff in any service the man attends need to be aware of the man's history if they are required to take specified precautions to minimise the risk of further incidents of abuse, for example, supervising the man or providing same sex intimate care. Their knowledge of the history does not need to be complete but it should ensure they are well informed about what situations constitute a risk of further abuse and **what they are supposed to do** about these.

On occasion there may be concern about an organisation's ability to deal usefully with a man's history, or to maintain an acceptable level of confidentiality. This is particularly so if it is proposed that a man accesses a voluntarily-run evening or holiday scheme because these are not always set up with the infrastructure to be able to store complex files and manage difficult behaviours. Where this is the case the solution is not to withhold the information but to reassess whether this is a service which can meet the man's needs without jeopardising others. Obviously the man may suffer if he is excluded from opportunities on account of his behaviour but his inclusion must be explicitly weighed up against the safety of other people who use the service.

activity 3c Sharing information

One particular dilemma is whether people with learning disabilities should be directly warned of the risks of abusive sexual behaviour. Refer to the scenarios in **Activity 3a: Service responsibility** to consider the following:

> **Gregory**
> *Gregory has a history of sexually harassing both women with learning disabilities and women staff. Staff at his group home think that his social isolation might be a contributory factor. In response to this they make arrangements for him to attend a social club for people with learning disabilities. No one at the club is told about his history. On the second occasion he attends, two women with learning disabilities who are regular participants are absent. A phone enquiry reveals that they are avoiding Gregory because he had said some rude things to them the week before.*

- Should women at the evening social club attended by Gregory have been told that if he said anything rude they could come and find a member of staff immediately?

> **Noah**
> *Within a large institution, Noah had gained a reputation for sexually exploiting less able people, who were often scared of what he might do if they tried to resist. Since he moved out of the hospital Noah has developed a relationship with a woman at the day centre. The staff who work with him are supportive of the relationship and are making arrangements for the two to have private time together. They have decided to keep his history confidential from the woman and her carers as they believe he should be given a fresh start now he is living in the community. One day his girlfriend complains that he forced her to have sex even though she was clear she did not want to.*

- Should the woman with whom Noah has struck up a relationship be offered any additional support?

continued...

Malcolm

Malcolm, an unemployed man, had grabbed a woman's breast at a local shopping centre. The police who apprehended him did not believe it was serious enough to press charges but referred him to social services because they thought he may have some sort of learning disability. Although Malcolm had not had any previous contact with learning disability services and seemed to cope with the practicalities of life with a little support from his family, it was suggested that he attends a day service for people with learning disabilities and that he receives individual counselling from the psychologist attached to the unit. Shortly after his arrival at the service, he was found to have taken sexual advantage of a number of less able and unassertive women with learning disabilities who use the service.

- Should service-users at the day service Malcolm is referred to be given any advanced notice that their new colleague might be difficult?

activity 3d   Sharing information: 'Need to Know'

Victor

Victor has lived in a large group home for a number of years. On at least three occasions during this time he has been found forcing himself sexually on less able people – both women and men. It was clear that in no way was this contact invited. Recently he has started a relationship with a woman who lives at another group home but whom he sees at the day service. On a couple of occasions he has invited her to his house in the evening. When this took place staff were very careful not to leave them alone because they were afraid he might take advantage of her despite the relationship appearing mutual. Now he has been invited to her house and his staff are worried about what supervision will be available there and whether they should say anything.

- Would you inform the staff in the woman's group home about Victor's history of abuse?

- Would you want the woman herself to be informed about his history?

- Would you want the woman's parents to be briefed about the developing relationship including giving them information about his history?

Using our guidance for Victor in **Activity 3d** we would expect the woman's service to be warned of Victor's sexual behaviour prior to visiting her home. This is because he will be entering a service where there are other vulnerable people – not just his girlfriend – who might be sexually exploited in this situation. The issue of whether the woman herself and/or her parents are informed is more difficult. With respect to the woman, before any service sanctioned any private time together it would be necessary to ensure that she had a good understanding of sex, in particular the issue of consent and that she felt able to discuss such issues with individual staff members. These safety measures would be more important than her having specific knowledge of her boyfriend's history which she may neither understand nor be able to act upon. One strategy would be to encourage the man himself to inform his girlfriend, but this is unlikely to happen. The parents would need to be informed of the risks at the point where there was any possibility of them providing opportunity for sexual contact between the two, however inadvertently, particularly if the woman's service was of an opinion that she was, as yet, unable to assert her decisions about sexual relationships.

Disclosure of the man's history is likely to prejudice many people against the relationship which may ultimately lead to its termination – maybe by the woman herself though most probably by her carers. This may seem hard on the man but it is worth considering how you would respond yourself to the possibility of a relationship with a man who has a history of sexually abusing, or if a member of your family were concerned.

Being held accountable

If an incident of abuse has occurred, the first person that services should be accountable to is the victim. This accountability may be forced upon a service if the victim (or possibly a relative or advocate) complains directly to the service as was the case when the parent of the child who was abused by Mr B called on his group home. Most often this accountability is haphazard but sometimes it will be formalised by the lodging of an official complaint or by the involvement of the police.

Elsewhere we have shown how the responses services make to men with learning disabilities who sexually abuse are often determined more by the status of the victim than the nature of the act (Thompson, 1997b). It follows then that services are made to take differing degrees of responsibility depending on who the victim is. In practice this means that services will be most under scrutiny when children or women in the general public are abused. At the other end of the spectrum services may feel little pressure to take responsible actions in the face of abuse of other people with learning disabilities or women staff. This discrimination was vividly illustrated in a recent independent inquiry into the circumstances surrounding the absconding of a man from a learning disability hospital who had a history of sexual assaults against children (Horizon NHS Trust, 1997). The inquiry's brief was to consider whether 'the public' – in particular children – were exposed to undue risk. It virtually ignored the ongoing risk of sexual abuse to people with learning disabilities who had no choice but to live with him – there was no independent inquiry for them.

Services clearly have multiple responsibilities in these circumstances. They may find themselves responsible for someone harmed in a previous assault, for the man himself and for **potential** victims. A helpful maxim is that the service should primarily be accountable to **the man's next victim**. This will ensure that prevention is not lost as a component of any responsive strategy.

Because of the lack of accountability, services can make inept responses over many years without much comment or interference. We saw above how services could hide behind confidentiality. By ensuring as few people as possible find out what a man with learning disabilities has done, the chance of complaint is minimised. This strategy is easiest when the victims themselves have learning disabilities. The propensity for services to deliberately conceal abuse against people with learning disabilities should not be underestimated.

Fortunately, progressive services are seeing the benefits of increasing openness about the lives of their clients, and are more open to being questioned about the steps they take to prevent men with learning disabilities from sexually abusing. The key to this step forward is providing information about the abuse and the steps which were taken to avoid it to people who are in a position to challenge the service. It may be further necessary to accompany this information with guidance on how to make a complaint against the service. People who should ideally be provided with the information would include:

- the victim
- their advocate (for example, parent)
- the purchasers of the service for the male abuser and that of the victim.

One service which was prepared to address its shortcomings in managing men with learning disabilities who sexually abused, established a multi-disciplinary advisory group to which it was additionally accountable.

We return to the issue of accountability in **Section 3.4** when we consider the interlocking system of agencies and the checks and balances built into the wider service system. First we need to consider what actions can be instituted which are effective and ethical.

See:

Case checklist G: Degree of responsibility
Case checklist H: Informing other services of risks
Case checklist I: Sexual risk disclosure sheet

part three

section
2 A Range of Responses

I n this section we look at a range of possible **responses** which
can be made to the men's behaviour, at how effective they are and
at the practical and ethical issues each raises. Possible responses
include those which focus on trying to change the behaviour and
the man's control over it, and at responses which seek to minimise
the harm he does to others. Responding in an area as controversial
as sexuality can never be easy. We have already documented the
difficulties of knowing for sure what the man has done, how accurate
the records are, how far he is responsible for his actions and how
difficult it is to balance his rights with the interests of other people
(especially other vulnerable people) who might be harmed by him.
Ethical consideration should always be built into decision making in
this area of our work. Decisions need to be transparent and open to
scrutiny in order to ensure that the needs and interests of the different
people involved are properly weighed up.

We have also rehearsed different ways of thinking about abuse
and of understanding its origins. We know that some people will
think in terms of punishment or sanctions, some will work on the
basis of teaching/learning and others will consider treatment or
therapy. These approaches overlap and interlock. For example, one
factor we noted which allowed men with learning disabilities to fail
to appreciate the seriousness of their behaviour was that responses
and sanctions have been so infrequently and inconsistently applied
to them. Men might have learned to stop what they were doing if
the responses had been immediate, clear and firm. Nevertheless we
see these three approaches as deriving from different professional
backgrounds and traditions within learning disability services and
will explore them now. At the end of this section we bring them
together by demonstrating how these different responses could be
brought together into a coherent management plan for each man.

The Criminal Justice System

Many men with learning disabilities who sexually abuse run the risk of contact with the legal system: either the criminal law or mental health legislation. The overall picture is of the legal system being unwilling to involve itself in the behaviour of people with learning disabilities, but when it does happen the consequences for the men can be very severe. This lack of consistency on the part of the legal system is a real challenge to services which are struggling to manage the men's behaviour. In particular it provides a huge ethical dilemma as to whether the police should be involved, because of the uncertainty of what this might lead to. Services then struggle with their own ambivalence as to whether to contain and minimise the man's conduct or risk exposing him to the vagaries of the criminal justice system (Clare & Carson, 1997).

In some cases the service itself will have no control as to whether the police are involved when a man with learning disabilities sexually abuses. This is typically the case when men abuse children or members of the general public. In other situations, services do sometimes decide not to report it to the police, even if this is stipulated in multi-agency procedures. If the matter does come to their attention, the police then have the choice about whether, and to what extent, they become involved. Prior consultation with the police, joint training (Stein & Brown, 1995) and a system of designated officers for vulnerable adults should be in place as a routine part of the adult protection remit and such links are hard to establish during a specific investigation. Problems should be fed back through a multi-agency group so that any deficits are ironed out before another case emerges from the woodwork.

Nevertheless, at the time of an incident, practitioners have to make an immediate decision about contacting the police and need to weigh up the following factors.

For	Against
A crime has potentially been committed so this is the appropriate course of action	The ultimate consequences may be disproportionate for the nature of the offence committed, for example indefinite institutionalisation
Not to call the police may suggest to the man involved that what he has done is not serious	The lack of action on behalf of the police, or a decision by the Crown Prosecution Service not to proceed, may serve to reinforce to the man that his behaviour is above the law. This is often a problem when men abuse other people with learning disabilities or are living in institutions
The consequences of involving the police may serve as a useful deterrent to future abuse	The abusive behaviour may be best managed by local services, particularly if the man has severe learning disabilities
It demonstrates respect for the experience of the victim	

Overall we believe it is important to register the men's behaviour as crimes, thereby exposing the legal system to the requirement that they respond effectively to all members of the community. Keeping men away from the legal system serves to insulate *it* as well as *them* from the need for change.

Moreover, there are safeguards for people with learning disabilities when they are investigated by the police in connection with possible crimes; specifically, there is the role of the appropriate adult which is designed to offer support, information and mediation between the person and the officers in charge of the investigation (Brown & Egan-Sage, 1996).

An appropriate adult may be anyone with experience in the field of learning disability and does not necessarily have to be someone who knows the person. Good services are recognising that training is vital to service this role (Mencap & The Law Society, 1995).

Most contacts with the police for men with learning disabilities do not lead to prosecutions but the police may still be able to play a part in helping the men understand how unacceptable their behaviour is. The experience of the police being involved may have taught the men that what they had done was serious.

Informal sanctions

One crucial strategy to minimise the possibility that a man will continue to abuse is to ensure that appropriate sanctions follow all incidents of abuse. By a sanction we mean a consequence which an individual would experience as undesirable but from which they could be helped to learn. This might include:

- temporary suspension from a service
- the withdrawal of desired activities
- increased supervision
- contact with the police.

Very reasonably, there is a lot of concern about services 'punishing' people with learning disabilities and many services reject it as an approach to working. Approaches to other sorts of challenging behaviour, often involving less able service-users, emphasise:

- working with their behaviour rather than against it
- discovering what it is they are trying to achieve (its function)
- trying to design approaches which will help them to achieve their goals by structuring learning and providing assistance.

However, when sexuality is the issue the matter is not as easy. If the function of a behaviour is sexual gratification at another person's expense then it has to be contained and redirected.

Punishment has a long and ignoble history in learning disability services. There is a history of workers acting abusively towards clients – sometimes in the name of behaviour management, sometimes on the basis of wholly inaccurate diagnoses or assessment. People have been punished for things which they could not control (for example, having erections or wet dreams) or from which they could not learn. Punishment of people with learning disabilities has often escalated and taken place behind closed doors, without scrutiny or challenge. Punishments have often been excessive and harmful as well as futile.

We want to distinguish between careless responses which are unplanned and idiosyncratic, and those which are part of a comprehensive care plan. Furthermore, we see the primary goal of sanctions not as a way of *seeking revenge* for what the men have done, but to help them *understand its seriousness* and avoid the kind of sanctions which would be applied if they were not sheltered by learning disability services, that is prison or other confinement.

Hence we also argue that the planned use of appropriate sanctions is ultimately in the men's own best interests, because if their behaviour continues unchecked they will be unable to remain within services or community settings.

Of course there are other potential benefits, most notably if sanctions prove effective in limiting the abuse of other people.

It would be preferable if the men's behaviour terminated because of their understanding of its impact on other people (Waterhouse, Dobash & Carnie, 1994, p252), rather than to avoid consequences for themselves. This might be held as a long-term aim but it is not unusual for men with learning disabilities to have limited empathy for the feelings of others, since empathy is actually quite a complex cognitive skill. Realistically, they will more likely be motivated to change their behaviour if they know it will mean missing out on things they want for themselves and if they are clear that this will happen if they persist in offending.

Selecting sanctions

In the table below, we list a range of sanctions which have been suggested as responses to sexually abusive behaviour, all of which were intended to help the perpetrator understand that his behaviour would not be tolerated by the service.

Table 3: Possible sanctions
■ Clear statements from staff that the behaviour is unacceptable
■ Staff limit positive communications with the man – remaining 'cold' for a while
■ Exclusion from day service for a limited period
■ Prevented from attending social activities
■ Supervised when out in the community
■ Enjoyed activities suspended. (For example, visits to friends or parents, shopping, walks, swimming.)
■ Stern warning/informal caution from the police

In selecting appropriate sanctions it is important to have as many different view-points as possible and to tailor-make the sanction to fit the man and what he has done. For example, there is no point in excluding a man living with his family who has a limited memory span from his day service for six weeks. He will have forgotten what he was excluded for in that time and it is likely that his family will have been punished more than he has. Careful thought will need to be given even to the form of words used so that they have the most impact on the man. It is no use being vague or long-winded – he will not get the message. If the police are involved they will also have to be briefed about how best to make the caution work for the man given his level of understanding; it might be that otherwise the police are too 'nice' to the man and that he ends up feeling special rather than admonished.

There is no reason why the man himself should not be given an opportunity to give an opinion where communication allows this. Although he may resist any sanctions being applied, the process of involving him in the discussion may be a start to helping him take some responsibility for his behaviour. For best learning, sanctions chosen should reflect 'natural consequences' to the men's behaviour, which rarely happens other than in those rare cases when men with learning disabilities face criminal prosecution for their sexual abuse. For example, a discussion like the one below might be beneficial for Mr D:

Worker:	We are very worried about you playing with yourself when staff are helping you in the bathroom.
Mr D:	(*silent*)
Worker:	Is playing with yourself a good or bad thing to do?
Mr D:	Good?
Worker:	Yes, it is good if you are by yourself. Where is a good place to do it?
Mr D:	In bed.
Worker:	Yes, bed is a good place to do it if you are by yourself. Where else?
Mr D:	Bathroom?
Worker:	Yes, but only if you are by yourself. Is it good or bad to do it when staff are helping you?
Mr D:	(*smiling*) Bad.
Worker:	Yes, you can only do it when you are alone in the bathroom. The staff don't want to see you do it. Do you think the staff want to see you play with yourself?
Mr D:	(*smiling*) No.
Worker:	No, they don't like it. They get upset. What do you think we should do if you do it with the staff again?
Mr D:	Don't know. I won't do it again.
Worker:	You've said you won't do it again before, but you still do it. What should we do if you do it again?
Mr D:	Tell me off?
Worker:	We've tried that before and you still do it.

In selecting sanctions the following should be considered:

■ Will he know that a sanction has been applied? For example, a man might be removed from a day service but because of his home situation, an alternative placement may need to be found. The man may not find one service very different from another.

■ Will it be experienced negatively by the man himself? A common problem is that some men with learning disabilities enjoy the attention their behaviour is afforded.

■ Will the man be able to connect the sanction to his abusive behaviour? If not, there are no grounds to apply it, and/or work may be needed to ensure that he is able to make the connection.

■ Does the sanction reasonably reflect the seriousness of his behaviour?

■ Can the sanction be consistently applied? For example, if it is decided that when a man exposes himself in public he will be directly returned to the group home, consideration needs to be given to whether this is practical if he is accompanied by other residents.

■ How long should it be maintained? This should be determined by thinking how long he will be able to make the connection stick in his mind.

Whatever sanctions are selected, they should never deprive the man of essential food, drink or clothing, or involve physical or emotional abuse. Furthermore they should never be left to the discretion of individual staff, but be agreed at a team meeting with the approval of the manager of the service and with multi-disciplinary input. Psychologists are often best placed to advise in the selection of appropriate sanctions and should be consulted. Detailed records should be made, mandating the service to put any decisions into action and also recording when sanctions have been applied in line with this plan. Programmes should be reviewed regularly and changed if staff have doubts as to their effectiveness.

Telling the man about the sanctions

As we said above there is no point in applying any sanction if the man is not able to link it directly to the unacceptable or abusive sexual behaviour. This might be done in anticipation of the behaviour or immediately afterwards when it will be possible to link the action of staff with the discovery of the man's abuse.

Sanctions are much more easily identified and applied to behaviour which happens on a regular basis and is consistently discovered. Where the man's behaviour is predictable and staff are waiting for it to happen again, it is important to plan the response to the next incident and to try to help the man understand in advance what this response will be. With some men this will not be possible because of their communication difficulties. Others may be helped to comprehend this connection using resources such as line drawings of the offending behaviour and a visual image of the consequence. In most cases it will be possible to inform the men of the threatened consequence verbally or with the use of signs or other communication aids.

To maximise the possibility of men linking continued unacceptable or abusive sexual behaviour with the chosen sanction it should be imposed as soon as possible after the behaviour and work should take place with the man to try to ensure he understands why it is being applied.

A common pattern for men with learning disabilities who receive some sanction for their abusive behaviour is for the behaviour to temporarily cease, and then a few months later for more incidents to emerge. There are a number of possible reasons for this. The man may have forgotten the consequence itself or have lost touch with the negative experience of it having being applied. Alternatively, the man may believe that staff are less attentive to his behaviour and that he may be able to escape detection or sanctions if he re-offends. To guard against this pattern it is necessary to keep reminding men with learning disabilities of the consequences they have received, why they came about and to repeatedly warn them of the potential future consequences. This 'maintenance' work may be necessary for a number of years and is perhaps one of the biggest challenges to services given the turnover of staff and the pressures for all concerned to move on and forget the incident.

Education

Sex education is often prescribed for men with learning disabilities who have sexually abused. In **Part Two** we saw how rarely the problem is the men's lack of understanding of what is right and wrong. The 'sex education' which is most likely to be most beneficial would ensure the following:

- the man knows his behaviour is abusive

- the man links his abusive behaviour to any sanctions which have been applied

- the man understands how his behaviour impacts on other people, particularly his victims

- the man knows what consequences may result from future assault.

The work should begin with some assessment of his knowledge of these points. Visual resources such as images of consented and unconsented touch are very useful for this work (McCarthy & Thompson, 1998). More detailed assessment, including attitudes to women and sexual interests require psychometric instruments and tests (Clare, 1993). These tests should be carried out by a qualified and experienced psychologist and not tried in a DIY fashion within services.

Treatment

A number of treatment options are available although many have a poor prognosis and are ineffectively evaluated or monitored. We have already showed how blurred the lines can be between treatment, punishment and control. However, the specific focus of therapy and treatment should be on procedures which seek to enhance the man's own ability to control his behaviour and will usually consist of cognitive and behavioural work, psychotherapy, or medical interventions.

There are clearly ethical issues about any of these interventions and the means do not always justify, let alone achieve, the desired ends. Regardless of the type of treatment it is important to ask on what ethical basis the treatment is proceeding. Often the practitioner covers him- or herself by arguing that the man with learning disabilities has given his informed consent but the validity of this consent does need to be challenged just as we had to challenge the validity of the men's consent to join in our research study (Brown & Thompson, 1997a). We think it is more important for the practitioner to work through the issues with others involved in the man's care and/or with an independent advocate and to assure themselves that, when the benefits and risks are weighed up, together with the benefits and risks of doing nothing, the intervention is in the man's best interests.

Treatment options include the following:

■ pharmaceutical interventions

■ psychotherapy

■ cognitive and behavioural treatments.

Pharmaceutical interventions

It is not unusual for men with learning disabilities who have some form of unacceptable or abusive sexual behaviour, like Noah in **Activity 3a** (page 99) to be prescribed medication which is intended to reduce this abusive behaviour. The one most commonly used in the UK is CPA or Androcur. Other men who have histories of abusing receive such medication less commonly. It is as if sexual suppressant medication is a first resort for men with learning disabilities and a last resort for other men, even convicted sex offenders. For this disparity to be justifiable one would need to be convinced that the other options which are put in place for other men are not relevant or effective for men with learning disabilities, an argument which would be difficult to uphold. The reasons why this discrepancy is so worrying centre on the following:

- the sexual behaviour of men with learning disabilities is often seen as a medical problem, where for other men it is regarded as a social and/or criminal issue

- studies are not conclusive about whether such medications are effective

- the potential side effects of sexual suppressant medications are particularly concerning – they include weight gain, breast development and liver problems

- the medication's effect on the sexual response system inhibits the possibility for satisfying masturbation or consented sexual relationships.

Clinicians pay poor attention to the legal requirement for men with learning disabilities to give informed consent to the medication.[1] One paper (Cooper, 1995) suggested that it was in fact not possible for men with learning disabilities to give informed consent to a sexual suppressant medication and looked forward to a time when, for ethical reasons, it was seen as no longer acceptable to sanction such treatment.

Informed consent is deemed to be problematical on a number of grounds. Firstly, because of cognitive difficulties, but also because the men who use services experience considerable pressure in relation to powerful professionals regardless of the particular pressure which may be applied in situations when an offence has been committed. It is difficult for a man to make a free and informed choice when effectively he may be being told 'you won't be able to go out alone if you don't take it'.

This does not yet help Noah (**Activity 3a**) who, like many other men with learning disabilities, has a medical practitioner who is reluctant to withdraw the medication. Because of the ethical problems outlined above, the onus should be on the doctor to demonstrate its efficacy if the medication is to be *continued* rather than on the staff team to take responsibility for its *withdrawal*. Ideally, the professionals should work together in a multi-disciplinary team to evaluate the outcome of Noah's treatment and produce a risk management strategy which they can all support.

---

1 This is not a requirement if the men are detained under mental health legislation specifically because of their abusive sexual behaviour.

Psychotherapy

Psychotherapy for men who abuse aims to affect the possible emotional origins of abusive behaviour – whether conscious or unconscious. There are a number of different schools or styles of psychotherapy, some of which have been explored in relation to people with learning disabilities (Sinason, 1992), including specific work with men who sexually abuse.

As with medication it is necessary to ask whether a man with learning disabilities who has sexually abused is making an informed choice about participating in psychotherapy. There may similarly be problems in understanding what psychotherapy involves – any therapist would agree that it is much more complex than 'talking about your problems'. The likelihood of some pressure from the referring agency, if not the therapist themselves, to attend sessions also militates against the possibility of valid consent. Although talking treatments like psychotherapy or counselling seem relatively harmless they are not without risks which the man should understand if he is to give proper consent. They include:

- the work may help the man get in touch with quite disturbing and even traumatic emotions

- behaviour may get worse

- disclosures of further abusive behaviour may emerge during the sessions which, when passed on by the therapist may result in more punitive sanctions.

As psychotherapy can offer no more convincing evidence of its efficacy than medication, it is important that the extent of these risks is taken into account when it is being considered for an individual man with learning disabilities. On the other hand it may also be a way of offering additional support to a man to come to terms with his behaviour and his history.

Cognitive and behavioural treatments

Cognitive and behavioural treatments are most often undertaken by psychologists. They involve working with the man and those who make up his environment to change his thinking and/or behaviour. These may involve a package of programmes including sex education, contracts, anger management, and social skills to reduce isolation. Potentially, these may also include attempts to alter the man's sexual arousal but, as was pointed out in **Part Two**, this is very resistant to change. It is not necessarily the case that these are easier for men with learning disabilities to make informed decisions about, compared to psychotherapy or medication. Again the service will probably exert some pressure to comply, and the risks are not easily understood. As with any face-to-face work, there is a risk that the men will disclose other sexual behaviours – the consequences of which may be experienced negatively. Furthermore, although such work may not be intended to be psychotherapeutic, it is impossible to control the emotional impact it may have.

Supervision and chaperoning

The goal of supervision is simply to prevent further abuse. It arises in situations where the risk to others is high and where the service cannot afford to let the man abuse again. It is predicated on an assumption that the man cannot or will not take responsibility for his actions. It is inevitably intrusive for the man, demanding for staff and costly for the service.

Supervision may simultaneously operate as a sanction and a deterrent from future abusive behaviour. Consider, for example, a man committing offences whilst out unaccompanied in the community who is subsequently prescribed a period during which he is not allowed out by himself. The experience of the supervision is likely to be experienced negatively and may provide some motivation for him to resist re-offending even if it is deemed safe to lessen the supervision.

part three

section

3 Drawing Up Care Plans

Bringing these elements of a programme together is essential if men with learning disabilities are to receive tailor-made responses, which are appropriate to them, to what they have done and to their level of responsibility and understanding. Drawing up the programme is the first step, but it is much harder to ensure that it is implemented within services over the longer term. This may be directly or indirectly due to a lack of resources but may also reflect a basic lack of commitment from key workers or agencies. Services may initially be keen to address the problems – they may have been convinced that something needs to happen but are often looking for simplistic solutions and a 'quick fix' which requires little effort on their part. Similarly, professionals who come into the service to offer advice should never underestimate the importance of the day-to-day work by seeming to provide 'hit and run' solutions; they may also need to be around to see how their ideas work out in practice and what barriers there are in the actual day-to-day living and working environment.

When it comes to evaluating the effectiveness of a programme, practitioners often confuse two different questions (Hogwood & Gunn, 1984):

- Was it actually implemented?
- Did it work?

Sometimes, programmes which might have worked are discarded because they have never been properly put into action.

The Care Programme Approach (Department of Health, 1996) is a common planning system in mental health services. It aims to ensure that services to an individual are co-ordinated and 'seamless'. Many people with learning disabilities are not benefiting from this system.

Valuing People (Department of Health, 2001) emphasises *person-centred planning* and *person-centred approaches* for people with learning disabilities. The need to prevent the life opportunities of men with learning disabilities being needlessly restricted because of the consequences of abusive behaviour should be placed at the centre of such approaches.

We look at the wider service system in **Section 3.4** but for the moment we will concentrate on what an individual care plan would look like for the men we have been concerned with.

The plan will look very different depending on the man's ability, the service context in which he lives and spends his time, and the behaviour he presents. Here we look at five different 'categories' drawn up to address a range of behaviours and risks:

- violent abusers

- men who are exploiting more vulnerable service-users

- men who abuse or expose themselves to staff

- men who are a risk outside services to members of the public

- men whose abuse is indirect or unintentional.

These are not rigid categories and you may be working with a man who falls between these examples or combines elements of several, but we hope they will provide useful exemplars as a guide to the types of responses which might be appropriate and effective. First we review some of the factors associated with each kind of abusing and the patterns of response which have emerged in the literature as well as in our study.

Violent abusers

This is the most serious category of abuse, because of both the man's intentions and the harm it causes the victim. Often these situations do not come to light until some time has elapsed because the man intimidates the victim to maintain their silence after the assault. They may also have chosen someone whose communication is limited and who will find it very difficult to report what happened to them. Many men with and without learning disabilities pick up on this vulnerability and so specifically target less able people for their assaults. Feminists have argued that the motivation for such assaults is as much the abuse of power as notions of sexual satisfaction.

Defining characteristics

Fortunately this type of abuse is rare in learning disability services but may be evidenced by:

- **Use or threat of force or weapon:** The victim is unable to avoid the assault because they are afraid of violence. The threat of violence may not always be direct because some men's reputation for violence means that at the time of the assault, threat is unnecessary. Victims may not resist because they fear worse consequences if they fight back (McCarthy, 1993). Because of this, any knowledge that a victim has about previous violence the perpetrator has exhibited should be understood as a background to the actual assault.

- **Knowledge of victim's dissent:** The man would have known that his victim did not want the sexual contact. For example, one man disclosed that the less able man that he had taken to the toilet over a number of years cried when he anally penetrated him. Another spoke of his preference to rape women who could not speak because they could not tell anyone.

Patterns

Men with learning disabilities who commit what are essentially serious sexual offences may abuse in this manner over many years. It may not come to light until the man abuses a member of the general public, when a pattern may emerge of prior assaults in learning disability services which have been denied or minimised (Swanson & Garwick, 1992). However, this tolerance is then abruptly ended and at some – to the man – apparently arbitrary point in time he is removed from his local environment, often to isolated services such as a specialist hospital. For many men with minimal learning difficulties, their abusing behaviour leads to their first encounter with learning disability services and by implication their diagnosis of 'learning disability'. The action also brings the men into regular contact with vulnerable people with learning disabilities – the risks of which are rarely recognised. Not surprisingly the men continue to sexually abuse in these new settings with fewer consequences because members of the public are not involved. Because these men are so able, their power over the other service-users may be such that they do not even need to resort to force in the process of sexually abusing. The consequence is that the men learn that they can get away with abusing people with learning disabilities, but will be punished if they victimise anyone in the general public. At the same time services feel that they have **succeeded** in controlling the men's behaviour, particularly because they are unaware of force being used against people with learning disabilities. Another point of view is that they have sacrificed their service-users to the men's sexual desires.

Clearly, if the victim remains silent about what has happened to them, or the abuse is not observed, the men's behaviour will be unchallenged. This is covered in the section on prevention which focuses on how services can enable people with learning disabilities to disclose abuse, as well as how changes in service structure can minimise the risk of this type of abuse.

Immediate responses

Perhaps more than any form of abuse, it is crucial that the first responses made when it is learnt that a man with learning disabilities has used force must reflect the seriousness of the crime that has been committed.

Police involvement

There should be no hesitation about contacting the police when men with learning disabilities use or threaten force when they sexually abuse. Possibly the victim themselves will initiate this or the service will have to act on behalf of other service-users. There are problems as to how far a woman with learning disabilities who has been assaulted should be given control over the involvement of the police. Her involvement might be needed if the case is to go to court, but the service has a duty to act on behalf of other service-users as well as this individual, and where there is a reasonable chance that such an attack would be repeated, or where it is part of a pattern of previous serious assaults, the service may need to override any hesitation on the part of a victim to report the matter to the police. Every effort should still be made to support the victim in the way they wish but not to let the course of any action rest on their shoulders. The problems with requiring the victim's consent before the service takes action include:

■ the time involved (which may cut across collection of evidence)

■ the risk that gaining their consent may undermine the integrity of any verbal evidence they could provide

■ the fact that services may have a hidden agenda to keep the problem in-house.

Increasingly, policy documents specify that the police will be consulted and/or involved as a matter of course.

Victim support

Providing immediate support for the victim will clearly fall to learning disability services when the victim is a service-user. A key responsibility is to ensure that the victim *is*, as well as feels, safe from their attacker. This can be most difficult to achieve if the two share a residential service. A very unsatisfactory compromise in small residential settings is to use increased staff supervision as a means of guaranteeing safety – if it is sustained it may offer safety but will do little to make the victim feel safe (or to validate their experience). An emergency case conference should be called as soon as possible as is usually recommended in local policies on abuse of vulnerable adults.

Response to the man

First ensure that the man does not have the opportunity to abuse again, or to make further threats towards the victim – he may try to frighten the victim into silence. Arguably this is a role for the police, and when the perpetrator lives outside services there may be little that can be done to control the man's movements. Where the man is a resident of services, it may be possible to exert greater control over him and it would be necessary to do so if he is sharing the service with the victim. Unless there are exceptional circumstances it should be assumed that the man must leave this service although this can be very difficult to arrange, not least if further risks to residents in the temporary setting are considered. Whether he is moved or not, increased staff supervision is likely to be necessary to assure the safety of other residents.

Briefing staff

Staff who come into contact with the man must be briefed as soon as possible about the manner in which they should engage with him. Very often in these situations staff are not told and/or minimise what the man has done and communicate to him that they believe he has been wrongly accused. Also staff may be keen to alleviate the anxiety that the abuse has raised – 'to make it better'. This may mean relating to the man in a way that suggests nothing has happened or sympathising with his plea that everything will soon be OK. At the other extreme staff may directly express their anger about what he has done, particularly when the abuse involved children. Although it may be healthy that the man gets a real sense of the outrage that other people feel, there is a fine line between this and being abusive towards the man. The key communication to the man should be that what he has done is very serious and decisions will have to be made about what happens to him. This should be reinforced by suspending the man's activities until they can be reviewed at an early care-planning meeting. For example, it would be very inappropriate if the day after the assault a man who had committed a violent assault went to the day centre as usual, or went on a holiday that had been planned for some time the following week.

Case conference

Whether or not the police are involved, an emergency case conference should be called as soon as possible. In the meantime someone should be sought to advocate on behalf of the man and to ensure that any actions that have been taken are properly explained to him.

Stewart's assessment and care plan

We have included the following case study to illustrate what a care plan might look like for a violent abuser.

Stewart

Stewart is one of the most able men who attend a day service for people with learning disabilities. A week ago staff heard crying coming from a storeroom, went in and found Stewart forcing himself sexually on a woman who also used the service. She was clearly in a state of distress and said afterwards that she had been dragged into the storeroom by Stewart and he had said that he would hit her if she told anyone. The staff at the centre were convinced that Stewart had forced the woman to have sex with him and that there was no relationship between the two. Further staff admitted that they themselves had been frightened by Stewart when he was angry.

The police were immediately involved and they took Stewart to the police station to be interviewed. They passed the results of their investigations to the Crown Prosecution Service but felt pessimistic that a prosecution would take place because the woman's learning disability and the difficulty she had being consistent about the events would make her a 'poor witness'. Stewart was immediately suspended from the day service and a week later a case conference was set up to decide his future management.

This was not the first time Stewart had been involved in such an assault. There was knowledge (but no clear information) of a similar attack on a woman a couple of years ago when he was living in an institution. He is now living in a group home with three other men where he has been for the last year.

Using **Finkelhor's model** set out at the end of **Part Two** (see pages 92–93) we developed the hypotheses shown overleaf about Stewart's behaviour.

A care plan is required regardless of the decision of the Crown Prosecution Service as to whether Stewart will face criminal proceedings. The probability is that their response will be not to recommend any action. If this is the case those responsible for the woman's advocacy should be made aware of the right to appeal and she should be given support to do so if that is judged to be in her best interests. We feel strongly that this course of action could also prove in the long-term to be in the man's own interest as it would demonstrate to him very clearly that his behaviour is against the law.

His care plan will collate a number of essential elements:

- suspension from the day service or from preferred daytime activities
- suspension from other activities
- ensuring safety of other people in his group home

- sanctions
- sex education.

Suspension from the day service

Because of the seriousness of the offence there is no justification for the man to return to the day service. To allow this would demonstrate to the man and his victim that such behaviour is not taken seriously by the service, and it would be very disrespectful to the woman concerned who has suffered trauma and distress, if she were to see her assailant on a daily basis. Some people with learning disabilities may 'cope' with the continued presence of a man who has seriously abused them. Usually this is because they will have had to survive similar experiences in the past, with obvious negative consequences to their self-esteem and expectations. Where services fail to take appropriate action they are confirming the victim's feelings of worthlessness.

Stewart has been removed from the service for three reasons:

- to impress upon him that his behaviour will not be tolerated
- to protect and show respect to the woman he attacked
- to protect any other vulnerable people in this setting.

The period of his suspension may need to be different to meet each of these separate aims. For him the immediacy of his removal is probably more important than its duration but for the woman he attacked and other vulnerable people at the centre he may need to be excluded permanently. Moreover, alternative day provision will have to be found: his group home is staffed on the basis that people will be out during the day. Alternative provision should take account of his needs as well as of the need to protect others; he may require one-to-one supervision in his new service. Care must be taken to try to ensure the new service is not experienced by Stewart as a reward for his violent abuse. Where alternative day provision is unavailable because of its absence or commitment of management, there should be advocacy made available to the woman he abused and to other members of the original day service to contest and/or contain his return.

Suspension from other activities

He should also be suspended for a period of time after the assault from other preferred activities – these may include access to other day activities like swimming, shopping, or evening clubs and social groups. Definitely this list should include any services which the woman he assaulted also attends. Exclusion could be permanent in order to protect her and Stewart should be made aware of this. An appropriate time period should be chosen by people who know Stewart and the service network. This would depend on appropriate arrangements being made for the safety of other service-users.

FINKELHOR'S MODEL FOR STEWART

Motivation to abuse	Overcoming internal inhibitors	Overcoming external inhibitors	Overcoming the resistance of victims
▪ Sexual feelings ▪ Beliefs that to be a 'strong' man you have to have sex with women	▪ Low self-esteem through broken attachments – no contact with family or anyone from the time before he moved to his current group home about a year ago ▪ Feelings that he has no control over where he lives or what services he accesses ▪ Limited concern about the response to sexual abuse: – staff at the day service have tolerated his verbal assaults on them and other service-users. They have also given only a verbal response to some physical assaults of other people who use the day service. There is the same pattern in the group home – probably he has committed such sexual assaults a number of times before without being detected – the known incident in the institution against the woman received a limited response – no prior involvement with the police	▪ Access to vulnerable women in the day service. Low levels of staff supervision – particularly at lunch time when the incident occurred	▪ Threatened to hit the woman. She will have seen (and possibly will have been a victim of) his physical assaults at the day service

Ensuring safety of other people in his group home

Stewart is known to have abused women in the past and is living in an all male house, although some of the staff are women. This does not necessarily mean that the men who share a group home with him are not vulnerable to sexual attacks – if indeed these have not already occurred. Indeed, it is a reasonable assumption that men with learning disabilities who sexually abuse women will also sexually abuse men (Thompson, 1994b). Regardless of whether the men have been sexually abused they have been on the receiving end of physical assaults from Stewart. The incident of sexual abuse should be seen as a trigger to review the safety of all people with learning disabilities with whom he shares a service. To this end it is essential to give the other men in the group home an explicit opportunity to complain about any of Stewart's behaviour towards them – the outcome of these enquires would help determine whether it is acceptable for Stewart to continue to reside in this group home or whether he needs a more secure and perhaps individual service. One outcome of such a review might be that increased staffing ratios are required. The reality in many services is that staff are aware of service-users who face unacceptable risks of abuse from the people with whom they share the services and that management or the purchaser cannot be convinced of the need to address this. If you are in this position, ensure you have raised your concerns in writing and try to find some way of alerting the advocates of the vulnerable service-users (particularly parents) of the risks. If Stewart does stay in the group home it will be necessary to produce written guidance for new or agency staff about the level of supervision they are to give him and how they should handle any difficult incidents; this guidance should be consistent with other service policies and should address the risks of physical as well as sexual violence.

Sanctions

Stewart will probably experience his withdrawal from his usual activities as negative sanctions but staff may also want to review other social activities, reduce opportunities for him to go out unescorted, or cancel a forthcoming holiday. For example, Stewart used to be a member of a swimming club which his victim also attended and which he enjoyed. Stewart was told he could not go back to the club at all although after several weeks he was allowed to go swimming early on a Monday morning when the pool was empty and far less exciting and he was accompanied by a male member of staff. The aim of this is to restate to Stewart the seriousness of his actions and to demonstrate to him that his world will not go on as normal.

Sex education

Work needs to be arranged with Stewart to ensure he understands the following basic points:

- it is very serious to try to have sex with someone who does not want it
- what has happened to him as a result of the last incident
- the potential consequences of a further incident.

As highlighted above it is essential that these points be revisited on a regular basis. There is no indication of a need for a broader sex education programme arising from the incident of abuse since this could not be traced back to any lack of knowledge on Stewart's part. If it was later seen that there were deficits in his sexual knowledge this work should be kept very separate and should be seen as part of his overall care management rather than part of the response to this incident.

Additional responses

Low self-esteem and social isolation are potential factors in Stewart's abusive behaviour, therefore the following options could be implemented, although they should not be seen as a soft option or a substitute for the steps outlined above.

Social skills work should prioritise finding and maintaining friends and not 'how to get a girlfriend'.

It should be recognised that counselling or psychotherapy would need to be long-term (a minimum of one year) to stand a chance of having any long-lasting benefit. Something like 'six sessions' is only likely to determine whether this is a viable way of working with him.

Mr E

Mr E was another man who fell into the category of violent abusers and his care plan followed similar lines. Although there was less direct evidence that Mr E had used or threatened violence when he was having sex with the less able man in the day centre's toilet, it would be naive to suggest that violence was not a factor in the abuse. This is because of his history of violence at the centre and the fact that the man he abused actively avoided him during the day. Therefore we would treat Mr E as a violent abuser with the same suggestions for police involvement, sanctions, and sex education. Because he lives with his elderly parents there is likely to be some resistance to suspending him from the service, as this would increase the stress on them. If this is the case, services would have to act creatively to ensure alternative provision was provided by, for example, employing a worker to stay with him in his own home to minimise the impact on his parents. It can be more difficult to apply sanctions when the men concerned still live in their family home rather than residential accommodation, because of the very different basis for the relationships with the carers. Parents may be very distressed by their son's behaviour and it is important that they do not end up being punished for his actions by having much needed services abruptly withdrawn. In the section on abuse which presents a risk to the public (see page 147) we suggest that it is sometimes necessary for a man with learning disabilities to move from the family home into residential services to maximise the possibility of challenging his abusive behaviour. Such a move should be considered for Mr E, not least because of the age and frailty of his parents.

One potential factor in Mr E's abusive behaviour was the physical and psychological impact of Prader-Willi Syndrome (see pages 63–64). Therefore his care plan should include counselling with him to ensure he has a good understanding of the syndrome and an investigation to see if treatment can be arranged for his undeveloped sex organs. There are two options which are widely used in the USA – hormone supplements and surgery. Gaining such treatment on the NHS would require specialist assessment and advocacy. Mr E should not be disadvantaged in seeking this as a result of his behaviour.

Men who are exploiting more vulnerable people

This is possibly the most difficult category for services to manage because of ambiguities about how far services should go to protect people from exploitative relationships. For men with learning disabilities to exploit the person they are having sex with requires them to have power over them. This means that the recipients are most likely to be other people with learning disabilities, although on occasion their victims will be children and this is dealt with separately below.

Defining characteristics

Presence of a power relationship that ensures the victim's compliance

Men with learning disabilities are relatively powerless people in society, so to sexually exploit another person they choose as victim someone who is even further disempowered, mostly other people with learning disabilities. These may be less able, but women of a similar ability to their male sexual partners are also easily sexually exploited (McCarthy & Thompson, 1997). For example, women with learning disabilities are known to regularly endure painful sex with their boyfriend because of the fear of losing him if they do not comply (McCarthy, 1993). Men with learning disabilities may have power over other people with learning disabilities as a result of the status they gain on account of money, employment, age or holding specific responsibilities. This category excludes power due to threats or use of violence (see **Violent abusers**, page 125).

Use of a person for non-mutual sexual gain

A power difference alone does not make a sexual contact exploitative. There is the possibility that the man does not take advantage of his greater power, and ensures that the relationship is mutually satisfying. Unfortunately there is little evidence to suggest that this often happens; instead there are many signs that men exploit the power they hold so that the less powerful individual has a less satisfactory experience. These signs include:

■ a person agreeing to sex in the belief it is a way to gain or maintain a relationship, as is the case with the woman who exposed Mr C's activities

■ the man having sex which is intended for his sexual pleasure irrespective of the experience of his partner. The partner's experience may actually be painful as is often the case for women and men with learning disabilities who are penetrated (McCarthy & Thompson, 1997; Thompson, 1994b)

■ the less powerful person not understanding the true motives of the man for the sexual contact. For example, a man dishonestly suggesting that if they agree to sex he will start a relationship with them or give them some payment. In other instances the less powerful person may believe that the sex signals a relationship with the man, but in fact the man would never entertain the possibility of having such a relationship with them because he does not value or respect the person. This is often the case when men with learning disabilities have some kind of sexual contact with less able people

■ there is some payment for sex. It is difficult to perceive of a situation where a person with learning disabilities who trades their body for some reward is in anything other than an exploitative situation. They do not share any common ground with the minority of prostitutes (both women and men) who articulate that they maintain control with their clients, and research has documented instances of women with learning disabilities working as prostitutes who were extremely disadvantaged when it came to getting paid or insisting their punters used condoms (Brown, Stein & Turk, 1995; McCarthy & Thompson, 1997).

Some may feel that describing sexual contact, which is anything other than mutual, as exploitative is too high a standard to apply. After all, 'normal' sexual relationships between women and men have often involved a degree of culturally condoned exploitation, with the woman believing she is there to satisfy the man's desires. Whilst this belief is diminishing within some western cultures, it is still prevalent amongst others and in many religions.

Legislation recognises that some power differences – including those that exist between adults and children – preclude the possibility of an acceptable sexual relationship. The new *Sexual Offences Act 2003* (see page 29) acknowledges the relative powerlessness of some people with learning disabilities in some sexual contexts. It says that it is illegal to have sex with people with learning disabilities where agreement is obtained by inducements, threats or deception. Therefore, because of power differences people with learning disabilities (like children) can meet a legal definition of being sexually abused even where they seemingly agree to the sexual contact. For a prosecutor, it is necessary to show that the perpetrator 'knows or could reasonably be expected to know' that the other person has a learning disability.

Patterns

There are two distinct situations in which men with learning disabilities sexually exploit other people with learning disabilities. These are within and outside of relationships. The relationships are almost always with women, who are the men's girlfriends or wives.

Sexual exploitation in relationships

People with learning disabilities are not unusual in their hopes of having a partner. However their commitment to this may be stronger than that of other people because of their difficulties accessing other symbols of social status; for example, having children, a job, a car, wealth, travel. Within relationships, sex carries particular meanings which may be very different for each partner. Traditional ideas give many women and men the understanding that sex is about meeting men's desires and men's pleasures: it is a service that women provide for their boyfriends. Another idea is that it symbolises love. On this basis a woman may have sex with her boyfriend to demonstrate her love for him. Some men have said that sex is why you have a girlfriend, and many women know that to refuse sex is to risk ending the relationship. Feminists have been very critical of these constructions of sex because they privilege the man's pleasure. This inequality is changing, and more women are demanding that their male partners pay attention to their pleasure. However, traditional ideas are still very prevalent and are widely held by people with learning disabilities (McCarthy, 1993) who may find it difficult to access new ideas through books and magazines.

It is clear from this that women with learning disabilities who both want relationships and do not appreciate that sex could be pleasurable for themselves, are vulnerable to sexual exploitation by their partners. Typically these women's boyfriends and husbands, whether they have learning disabilities or not, pay little regard to their experience. There is little reason to suggest that men without learning disabilities are unaware of their power in such situations and so their behaviour could always be regarded as exploitative. However this may not always be the case for men with learning disabilities which is why we made a distinction between those men who are insensitive and those men who are exploitative.

Talking to the man with learning disabilities himself may provide the most effective way of assessing how intentional he is in exploiting his power sexually. The man may be open about making threats to end the relationship if the woman does not agree to have sex, he may also acknowledge that there are aspects of the sex that she does not like or he might show that he believes the sex should be solely for his benefit. Other patterns of exploitation are expecting the woman to tolerate his behaviour outside the relationship which many people would see as unacceptable; for example, having another girlfriend simultaneously, or having sex with other people.

Sexual exploitation outside of relationships

Outside of relationships, men with learning disabilities may be required to be more resourceful in gaining the compliance of less powerful people to have sex. They may falsely promise to women that sex will lead to a relationship or offer some other inducement to have sex such as cigarettes. Even if the man does nothing it may be that the other person lacks the knowledge that they should be able to make a choice and the skills to exercise that choice. For example, many men with learning disabilities who are anally penetrated describe it as painful but in response do nothing other than to 'wait 'til it finishes' even when there are no threats or inducements to engage in this type of contact (Thompson, 1994a). In other situations the less powerful person may make assumptions about what will happen if they do not agree to the contact. This was illustrated in a TV programme about the sexual abuse of people with learning disabilities where a woman accepted sex because she was afraid she would lose her 'friend', who took her for trips out if she did not accept (the perpetrator in this case did not have learning disabilities and the courts failed to recognise this as evidence of abuse) (BBC 2, 1991). Another fear which may make people with learning disabilities agree to sex when they otherwise would not, is the risk of violence based on experience with other men, even where this is not explicitly threatened. If this is the case, not resisting the sex should be understood as a rational survival strategy with which many other victims of abuse can identify.

One way of gauging whether a man with learning disabilities is exploiting other people with learning disabilities is to look beyond the sexual contact to the interactions that exist between them on a day-to-day basis: does the man demonstrate care, interest, and reciprocity or is his contact limited to the sex and manipulation of the other person to have sex?

Factors which sustain this behaviour

Staff attitudes to sexual relationships

Staff have very different attitudes to sexual relationships where one partner is more powerful than the other. This diversity of opinion is most clearly illustrated when people with learning disabilities have sexual relationships with people without learning disabilities (most of whom are men). Some people see such relationships as a mark of progress (Fairbairn, Rowley & Bowen, 1995), whereas others regard them as almost invariably exploitative. Staff attitudes will also differ as to what degree of inequality is acceptable in the sexual experience. For example, staff have very different feelings about the acceptability of Mr C's sexual relationships. These may range between arguing that the woman is making a free choice to engage in sex with him, even though the experience is negative, to suggestions that she is not in a position to give informed consent to any sexual contact with him. There can be a much greater tolerance of what women should be expected to put up with in relationships with men, compared to sexual contacts between two men. For example, if Mr C's actual girlfriend complained about penetration being painful with him, she is likely to gain a less outraged response than a man with learning disabilities saying another man anally penetrated him and he did not like it. The former is more likely to lead to counselling for the individuals involved, the latter to an abuse enquiry. Where staff are neither challenging nor aware of exploitative sexual behaviour amongst people in their services, there is little chance for change.

Service design

Service design may facilitate sexual exploitation because of the mixture of people it brings together. This is most obvious when vulnerable people with learning disabilities are expected to share services with comparatively able men. These men's relative power in these circumstances is so great that they can easily exploit without any need to resort to threats or use of violence. Often women perceive these men as desirable boyfriends because of the status that their ability attracts. The men on the other hand are not likely to value the women, but may see benefits in using them for sexual gain.

Immediate responses

Sexual exploitation by men with learning disabilities as defined above does not always demand the involvement of the police as in the case of violent abuse. There are two factors which should help make this decision. These may be considered as part of vulnerable adult procedures which should always be implemented in these situations.

Firstly when the severity of the person's learning disability precludes any consent to sex. This would include their ability to make choices, to say no and to communicate what has happened to them. A useful test is whether, after a man has sex with a person with severe learning disabilities in a private space, staff can assess confidently the other person's feelings about it. If they cannot, the person should be considered too vulnerable to have a sexual relationship and the police should be involved.

Secondly if there is evidence of the person being targeted because of their vulnerability. This may be a pattern in the man's behaviour. Malcolm's case (**Activity 3a**, page 99) might fall into this category. It is a reasonable assumption that this is happening if the sex involves a man without learning disabilities, but it is also the authors' experience that it is usually the case when men with mild learning disabilities seek sex with people with more *severe* learning disabilities (Brown & Turk, 1992).

Other immediate questions to be addressed when there are signs of men with learning disabilities exploiting other people with learning disabilities are:

- Is the perceived exploitation serious enough to ensure the two people do not have any contact until an investigation clarifies the situation?

- Is medical attention required to investigate the possibility of pregnancy and/or sexually transmitted diseases?

In many cases of exploitation an immediate intervention is not required. Instead staff should take time to gain a greater understanding of the dynamics of the relationship, to clarify their colleagues' position on it and what action is appropriate to try to stop, challenge or minimise the exploitation. Such a measured response would be appropriate as a result of the woman who disclosed Mr C's relationship with her.

Care planning

The first step in care planning for both people involved is to make a decision about the service's attitude to the exploitative sexual behaviour and to see if it is thought to be

- unacceptable

- needing challenge and support, or

- tolerable.

Unacceptable

In addition to the situations which warrant immediate police involvement there may be others where the degree of exploitation is too great, as will be the case when there is a wide difference in ability. This may include situations where the less powerful person may be initiating or welcoming the contact. When this position has been reached it becomes the service's responsibility to ensure that the sexual contact does not continue. The strategies to do this include separating the individuals and increasing supervision. Where there are grounds to believe that the man was unaware of the undesirability of the relationship it may be appropriate to support him in addressing this. Unfortunately, even when services are clear that a man's sexual contact with less able people is unacceptable, they often fail to intervene in order to prevent this in the future. If necessary, the man should be warned that further sex along these lines will lead to sanctions such as his exclusion from a service; in other words, it is fair enough to accept that he might not have realised that his behaviour was exploitative but if that is the case he needs to be told and expected to take the message seriously.

Needing challenge and support

Where the ability levels of the people involved are similar and both are giving some kind of consent to the sexual relationship it is inappropriate to stop the relationship on the basis of exploitation – respect must be given to people with learning disabilities who make their own decisions and learn from their experiences. This is likely to be the situation in Mr C's case because the woman's toleration of painful sex is not unusual for many women without learning disabilities for whom overriding their decision to stay in the relationship would be unthinkable. In these situations the service should respond by ensuring support is available to the individuals involved. For the less powerful person this would include ensuring that they are aware of the inequalities in the relationship and their choices. For the man with learning disabilities who is exploiting, this support should similarly ensure he is aware of the inequalities but should also challenge him not to exploit his power. For example, Mr C should understand that there are aspects of the sex that the woman who made the disclosure does not enjoy and that it is disrespectful for him to suggest to her that she is his girlfriend when he publicly acknowledges another woman as his partner.

Support can take many forms. It could come from:

■ a sensitive key worker

■ women's or men's groups

■ assertiveness training

■ individual counselling or therapy.

If one forum is unsuccessful it may be appropriate to try another.

Tolerable

Often services need to accept that in sexual relationships involving people with learning disabilities there will be some exploitation of power which has to be tolerated. This may ultimately be the case with Mr C's situation if the situation does not change, despite work that challenges him on his exploitation and support to the woman involved.

The line between sexual contacts that services should regard as unacceptable and those which should be responded to with some kind of support is very difficult to fix. It is typical that staff will have very different opinions about this which can lead to some very confusing responses, as Tim's case study below demonstrates.

Tim

Tim was often found lying on top of and kissing a much less able woman with whom he shared a hostel. She welcomed that contact and would often try to initiate physical contact with him. Some staff would stop this contact either because they thought the shared lounge where it was taking place was inappropriate or they believed the woman was too vulnerable. Other staff would not intervene. Attitudes towards the possibility of them going somewhere more private were even more confused. Some people believed that the service should tolerate the public kissing, otherwise there was a danger that they would be forced to go somewhere more private where they might go 'further', whilst others felt that, as adults, this should be totally acceptable but would not 'stick their necks out' to allow this to happen.

As a consequence of the above situation staff had asked for Tim to have education on consent. In a way they were trying to leave the judgement about whether it was an acceptable relationship with the exploiter! What was clearly necessary was for staff to debate, and come to a consensus about, the relationship so that they could be consistent about it and explain their decision to the individuals involved.

Men who abuse or expose themselves to staff

Serious attention to this form of abuse is rare, and yet it is common and identified by staff as a problem (Thompson, Clare & Brown, 1997). Management responses tend to suggest that it is 'part of the job' for front-line workers. Overwhelmingly the victims of this form of abuse are women direct-care staff. It is interesting to note that staff's relative power over men with learning disabilities is shown to be so fragile when the men turn round and sexually abuse them.

Defining characteristics

Staff or carers targeted

The most likely victims of this form of abuse are the staff who work with them, or other people who have a support role in the men's lives. These may be family members, foster parents or volunteers. As is noted above, women are disproportionately represented in all these groups even allowing for their predominance in 'caring' roles.

Unwanted sexual attention

Typical forms of abuse are verbal harassment, touching women staff intimately, exposure and masturbation. What is common is the women's lack of consent to the sexual behaviour. Other forms of abuse may be more subtle and would include looking at women in a particular sort of way – 'leering' – being persistent in demands for a particular woman's attention, or men insisting that only women attend to intimate care tasks because of the sexual pleasure this provides them.

Patterns

Mr D's case study shows some of the common features of men with learning disabilities who harass or abuse staff. The most significant of these is that the men are **not** indiscriminate about who they abuse: they target women, often black or young women and often new staff. This is not necessarily a reflection of heterosexual orientation because work has shown how rare an exclusive heterosexual orientation is for men with learning disabilities (Thompson, 1994b). Instead, what seems likely is either that the men have learnt that women are less powerful within the hierarchy, or that sexual harassment of women is culturally more acceptable than that directed against men. Where men are making choices about who they victimise, it is reasonable to assume that they have control over whether they abuse or not, irrespective of the degree of their learning disabilities. Having control over their behaviour means they must take some responsibility for it.

Another common pattern found amongst men with learning disabilities who abuse staff in a variety of ways is their subtle attempts to erode the boundaries of the staff/client relationship. For example, a man with learning disabilities may start by sitting next to a woman staff member, holding her hand, but after some time may move his hand up her arm eventually touching her breast or caressing her hair. If the hand-holding is considered appropriate by the woman, it can be very difficult for her to determine at what point the touch became invasive and she may also feel responsible for allowing some contact in the first place. This ambiguity may not all lie with the man as services are also very confused about boundaries (Thompson, Clare & Brown, 1997; Brown, 1998).

Similarly, verbal harassment of staff, which involves the man asking staff explicit questions about sex, usually starts with relatively innocuous questions. The man may move from asking where the staff member lives to whether she has a boyfriend, to whether they have sex, and to finally asking whether he puts his penis in her vagina. Different staff will have different ideas about when such questioning becomes too personal and abusive. What is needed is a clear consensus and briefing and support for women staff members so that they are not left to deal with this as a personal choice but as a shared matter of professional practice. The staff group, including men, should question why the man might want to know such intimate information and, if his curiosity is judged to be genuine, to provide a proper forum for sex education. Is it because he is looking for answers which he does not know, or are the answers irrelevant to his pleasure in engaging women staff in talks about sex? It may be that providing a man for him to talk to, who will answer genuine questions but who will make clear that this is unacceptable behaviour, is what is necessary. There is no contradiction between services having a strong commitment to sex education and teaching men that they have no right to talk about sex whenever they want with whomever they want.

Some men harass staff in other ways that are not overtly sexual, for example, by constantly demanding attention where there is a risk of violence if these demands are not met. There may be an underlying sexual motivation to such behaviour, particularly if the behaviour is only directed at women staff. Such a connection would be very difficult to establish but the presence of this pattern does indicate a need to be very clear about setting boundaries between the man and his contact with women staff. We met one man who was an extreme example of this in our research.

Geoff

Geoff had a long history of developing intense relationships with women staff at the day service. As time went on he would make even more demands on their attention which inevitably they were unable to meet. When this occurred, he would become violent towards the woman concerned who would reasonably limit her contact with him afterwards. There was a succession of women who believed they had overcome this problem only to find themselves ultimately to be on the receiving end of his violence. The answer was not to hope that future women staff would succeed where previous workers had failed but to set strict limits on the contact he had with all women staff, and to recognise that it was totally inappropriate for his key worker to be a woman.

Immediate responses

Police involvement

Being a staff member or other carer does not remove women's rights to seek redress from the legal system if men with learning disabilities are sexually abusing them. Although the service should take the initiative in seeking to support a woman who has been victimised to this degree, it is ultimately her decision if she wants to involve the police and the service should not stand in her way.

Situations when it is particularly appropriate to involve the police are when the abusers are more able men who are both aware of the inappropriateness of their behaviour and would understand the significance of police involvement. There may also be times when it is desirable to use the law with less able men. This will be the case if they have used or threatened force in the process of the assault.

There is a danger that many staff will consider most forms of abuse against members of staff as trivial and not worthy the effort of police involvement. This is reinforced by the attitude highlighted above that staff should be expected to tolerate a certain level of abuse in their job. One way to minimise the effect of this censorship is to ask what an appropriate reaction would be if the man carried out the same form of abuse on a member of the general public.

Legal action is not limited to the man himself: where a service has unreasonably failed to either brief or support women workers they may take action individually or collectively against their employer under Health and Safety legislation.

Support for victims

Irrespective of the man's ability and intent in his sexual assault, staff may be distressed by sexual harassment or behaviour. In particular new staff may be unprepared for the kinds of sexual victimisation that other staff have become numbed to; for example, there is no reason why a women who is 'flashed' at by a man with learning disabilities should necessarily experience that any differently from a man in the street doing the same thing, especially if she has not been inducted into the work sensitively and has been told that intimate care will be a part of her job.

Support for staff should start by respecting their experience, rather than expecting them to be able to carry on regardless as some kind of proof of expertise or professionalism. Instead, what often happens is that individual women are blamed for leading the men on in some way (for example, unclear boundaries or the way they dress), or for their inexperience. Practical measures may include suggesting that they go home, or ensuring they are not left alone with the man until a time when a more consistent strategy can be developed. Since women bear the brunt of sexual assaults on staff, male managers and supervisors should be sensitive to this as an additional stress in the job. Often substituting male staff for this particular man will immediately ensure that other women are not exposed to harassment.

It is helpful to staff who are going to have to deal with sexual harassment from service-users to warn them of this possibility in advance where men have a history of such behaviour. Unfortunately, this often does not happen which makes new or agency staff particularly vulnerable as they are unprepared.

Response to the perpetrator

In most cases it is essential that the man immediately understands that his behaviour is intolerable. This may simply involve the staff member stating what the offensive behaviour is. For example, responding to intrusive questions by saying 'That is too private, I'm not going to answer those kinds of questions'. Less able people may not understand words but could pick up on gesture and manner – so the women who Mr D assaults in the bathroom may indicate their feelings by finishing the intimate care as quickly as possible, with minimum social interaction or eye contact.

Staff may initially react to the man very differently, possibly expressing their anger in a considered way. This does not imply that it is acceptable for them to do or say anything – there is a need for all staff who work with people with learning disabilities to be able to maintain some objectivity even in stressful situations.

Where men have committed sexual assaults against staff, services should be particularly alert to the possibility of the men's exploitation of service-users as well, and so any immediate response which is designed to protect staff should not leave people with learning disabilities vulnerable.

Care planning

Care planning for men who sexually abuse staff should focus on two main issues:

■ how the risk of assault or harassment can be minimised

■ what response the service should make to the recent abuse and any further assaults.

It is crucial that the problem is seen to be located in the behaviour of the man, and that this is addressed by the whole staff team rather than by being critical of the behaviour of individual workers. The gendered nature of care work and sexual harassment often means that male staff and managers who have not experienced such harassment first-hand can fail to empathise with their colleagues and remain unsympathetic.

Minimising risk

The primary way to minimise the risk of staff abuse is to limit the contact between the man and the likely victims; for example, if a man is persistent in abusing women staff during intimate care, a solution may be to ensure that his intimate care is only undertaken by men. In many services this is not practical because of the limited number of male staff working in them. If this is the case, the service may need to move towards a position where this is possible by examining their recruitment policy (the *Sexual Discrimination Act 1975* allows for the specific employment of women or men in such situations).

Mr D's care plan

The service in which Mr D lived did not allow for intimate care only to be undertaken by men so this was not a possibility in his care plan. However it was decided that, wherever possible, men would be responsible for this. This meant that sanctions needed to be worked out in advance for the possibility of continued assaults of women staff.

Consequences to future assaults:

Masturbation during intimate care

Women to say firmly, 'Don't touch yourself – you are not alone'.

Immediately leave bathroom, returning a few minutes later, and continue intimate care with minimum of contact. Additional sanction – routine of hot chocolate with staff before bed withdrawn that night.

Coming down stairs naked

Women to say firmly 'No – get dressed'.

Minimum contact for the next hour. Additional sanction of withdrawal of night-time hot chocolate. When he does not do this, positive reinforcement is to be provided in the form of extra attention at that time and immediately afterwards.

Sex education

Individual sessions to be arranged with the aims of ensuring he knows:

* that masturbation alone in his bedroom is good and that it is not good if someone else is there (using line drawings)

* what will happen if he either tries to masturbate during intimate care or comes down stairs naked.

Other potential aspects of the care plan

Although it is unlikely to have an immediate or direct impact on his abusive sexual behaviour, attention should be given to his broken attachments and current isolation by maximising contact with people he has known and by providing support to help him form and develop new friendships.

Men who are at risk, outside services, to members of the public

This group covers men with learning disabilities who, whilst out by themselves in the community, pose a risk of abuse to the general public. The more common forms of these behaviours are listed below including a description of how these are typically presented. Although research shows that the nature of the men's acts in these circumstances are usually significantly less intrusive than abuses directed at other people with learning disabilities, these are the kinds of behaviours which lead to the most serious consequences for the men involved (Thompson, 1997b). Members of the general public are both in a better position to complain about their assaults and to have them acknowledged by the legal system than is the case when people with learning disabilities are victimised. By separating this group out we do not want to reinforce the privileged responses received by members of the general public who are, with the exception of children, ironically usually considerably more able to take care of themselves than are many vulnerable service-users.

Sexual abuse of children

These crimes usually involve men with learning disabilities going independently to places where they believe they will see children, for example, parks and schools. The extent of the crimes is often limited to trying to touch the children in relatively public places. More intrusive crimes are rare because the men lack skills and resources which other child abusers use to develop relationships with children, take the children to more private places and ensure their silence. Also men with learning disabilities tend to be powerful only in comparison with very young children who are generally very well supervised by adults.

Exposure

This is typified by men with learning disabilities being seen exposing themselves or masturbating in public. The men may have tried not to be seen or to have acted deliberately in view of others. This group is distinct from less able men who never go out alone, for whom there is some possibility that they do not understand conventions of privacy.

Sudden attacks

Again this involves men with learning disabilities who are out by themselves. The attacks are typically directed at women and involve the man grabbing the woman in some way – possibly her breasts. Rarely do the men put much effort into not being identified – the attacks often happen very close to home and in full view of other people. Furthermore, it is rare that these assaults extend beyond the initial 'grab' because other people are around or the person themselves is able to prevent this in some way. Although this can be experienced as a shock by the victim of such an assault, the violence is not usually extreme.

Sexual harassment

This covers a range of behaviours including persistently contacting or following (stalking) individual women. It might involve the man hanging around a particular person's house when that person has made it clear that they do not want him there, or verbal harassment of women he knows or of strangers.

Patterns

With all the above behaviours there may be a pattern consisting of the man having committed a number of offences without occasioning significant consequences. The victims themselves may be forgiving because of the man's learning disability or they may feel that involving the police would be too much trouble. Where men were not previously in learning disability services such behaviour may have given rise to their first contacts with such services, for example, starting to attend a day service or seeing a psychologist. If the police are brought in, they may feel unable to do anything because of the man's learning disability. The reality is that although the men might for some time 'get away' with such assaults they stand a very real risk of being institutionalised indefinitely for future incidents. Moreover, these further incidents may not be any more serious than earlier assaults for which there was little response – the man may just happen to touch the child of influential parents or the local community's tolerance may be exhausted.

Sanctions

As with all types of abuse, the man needs to experience sanctions which demonstrate to him the seriousness of his behaviour. To fail to do so in the above circumstances is to undermine any understanding that the man may have that his behaviour is unacceptable and may ultimately lead to his removal from the community. One key sanction which should be considered when a man with learning disabilities poses risks when he is out alone is to consider 'grounding' him and not allowing him to go out by himself. This might appear very draconian and without any legal basis but the reality is that he runs a risk of indefinitely losing the possibility of going out alone – for example, if sectioned under the *Mental Health Act 1983*. Grounding him or insisting on chaperoning him when he is out should balance three objectives:

- to protect him from the consequences of further assaults, which could include losing his freedom

■ to signal to him how seriously his behaviour is being taken

■ to 'teach' him in a limited way and for a limited time what it means to lose one's freedom.

Recent mental capacity legislation in the UK has improved the legal framework within which it is possible to insist a man with learning disabilities does not go out alone if he is unable to take responsibility for his sexually abusive behaviour. Such a decision would need to be argued to be in his best interests before either the local Sheriff (Scotland) or Court of Protection (England). Formal proceedings provide an important safeguard for the man.

Services also have a 'duty of care' enshrined in law and it can be argued that a service would be failing in this duty of care if it did not take action which limited the risk of the man being institutionalised as a result of committing an assault, where there was a reasonable assessment that such an assault might take place. It is our view that suspending a man's access to the community is both a valid and important strategy to responding to abusive behaviour *in certain cases*. Often services are resistant to such a suggestion, either ideologically or because of the resource implications such action demands.

The acceptance of people with learning disabilities in the community is still very fragile, and it could be argued that there is a *decreasing* tolerance of people acting unusually in any way. This impacts significantly on men with learning disabilities, even if their sexual behaviour does not include serious sexual offences. Lesser behaviours, such as hassling women in shops for a relationship, sexual behaviours with animals, and wearing women's clothing in public might test public tolerance to its limits. We would argue that none of these behaviours should lead to long-term institutionalisation because of the limited victimisation of other people, but in many cases this happens because the local community is unable to cope with men acting in these ways. Although we are critical of the low tolerance of some communities, there should be consideration of the balance between the risks to the community if a man stays there and the risks to the man if he is put into an institution. Where tolerance is limited it may be necessary to use very clear sanctions to demonstrate the risks to the man even if you yourself do not consider the behaviour as particularly serious.

Mr B

Care planning for Mr B should include a period in which his access to the community is suspended. The duration should be long enough:

- to demonstrate the seriousness of the assault – anything under a month would be inadequate

- to develop a contract with Mr B about how he might spend his time when out by himself in future, and there should be some confidence of his adherence to this.

A particular problem with Mr B is his experience of having no control over where he resides and so it may take a long time to help him understand that his behaviour will determine whether he stays where he is or is removed to an institution. Furthermore, his low self-esteem may mean that he does not care enough about where he lives for this to be a useful contingency.

Generally we would not advise considering a man like Mr B be given free access to the community again until there was some evidence that he himself was willing to make some commitment to stopping further assaults. When this time comes, access to the community must be gradually reintroduced. To maximise the possibility of Mr B avoiding further incidents it would be wise to choose times when children are unlikely to be out, for example during school hours or in the evening, and to say that he must not go to parks by himself. Other places where Mr B's access should be very carefully considered would include swimming pools and routes or neighbourhoods near schools.

Sex education

The major component of Mr B's sex education would be to ensure that he understands that touching children is very serious, the consequences he has received because of this and the potential consequences of further assaults. Staff may be tempted to insist that he destroys his collection of pictures of children believing his use of them may increase the risk of further abuse. In such situations we are just guessing what the best strategy would be. Whatever choice is made, Mr B should understand that if he does have any pictures no one else would want to see them.

When Mr B does have a chance to re-access the community, he should have sessions which clearly delineate the places he should not go to and give him a plan for any time that he feels he is tempted to try to touch a child. This may be to come straight back home or to ring staff immediately.

Men whose abuse is indirect or unintentional

The final category, which fits Mr A's (see page 12) and George's behaviour (below), covers those men who show no intention to sexually abuse other people but possibly this is how their behaviour is perceived. Generally it involves men with severe learning disabilities who may have a limited understanding of privacy and boundaries of touch. We have called this group **indirect abusers** because, regardless of the motives of the man, other people may feel abused by it. This category also covers men whose behaviour we defined as inappropriate in **Part One**.

George

George, a man with severe learning disabilities, persistently tries to touch and remove his penis under his clothing. The motivation appears to be one of comfort and there is no evidence that he does it to offend other people or to gain their attention. This happens throughout the day – regardless of what activities staff are trying to involve him in. Staff do at times say to him 'Don't touch' which does stop him touching for a couple of minutes but then the behaviour resumes. The effect of this is that most staff have given up trying to stop him at home and concentrate their efforts on when he is out in public.

The difficulties of linking action to consequence are greatest for men like Mr A and George because of the severity of their learning disabilities. Although the situation with George looks intractable, this is not necessarily the case. We have encountered services which have successfully reduced the amount of such behaviour. We have encountered others which have failed to achieve this, the difference being more attributable to the energy the service is willing to put into addressing the behaviour than of the ability of the man himself. Below we describe the process by which George's residential service helped him to stop touching his penis publicly. The service had a good staffing ratio which allowed individual staff to work with George on a one-to-one basis for periods of one hour three or four times a day.

Developing George's care plan

As a base line, staff identified activities George particularly enjoyed. These included:

- eating
- modelling clay
- touching different fabrics.

Staff recorded the frequency of George touching himself during favoured activities without any intervention. This turned out to be at least once every two minutes.

Four staff were assigned to work one-to-one with George for ten-minute slots, about five times a day, involving him in one of his favourite activities. Attempts to touch himself were consistently responded to during this time with 'Don't touch' and a physical prompt to remove his hand if necessary. At other times of the day prompting continued, but it was recognised that because of demands on staff time it was likely to be less consistent.

After three weeks George appeared to have associated the ten minutes one-to-one time with not touching himself. The touching reduced to, at most, twice in a ten-minute session. Work continued as before.

After a further three weeks, George only touched himself on average once every two sessions. Outside these times staff believed that his touching had reduced and they said they only had to look at him to stop him from touching himself. Sessions continued as before but with staff staying with George for half an hour.

Two months after sessions started George was averaging only one touch every three sessions, and staff noticed if they started the session by saying 'Don't touch', he was unlikely to try to touch himself at all during the session. This started to generalise outside the times of the sessions, particularly when he was in the company of staff who had spent time with him in the one-to-one situation. Because of the connection he seemed to have made between the individual staff and the behaviour, a wider group of staff became involved in the session time.

Four months after the beginning of the programme, George's touching was reduced to less than once an hour, and staff could be very confident that if they paid him close attention he would not try to remove his penis from under his clothing.

It appeared that the only consequence that George required was a hint of disapproval from the staff who worked with him. Note that the programme was very dependent on having staffing which allowed frequent one-to-one sessions with George. Services which are unable to provide this level of support are unlikely to be able to achieve significant changes in this type of persistent behaviour. If this is the case it is important to recognise that the problem lies more with the service than the man himself. The improvements with George were sustained, but any future changes in service or staffing levels may cause the behaviour to re-emerge. If this happens it will be useful to be able to refer back to the success of the above programme, to demonstrate that his touching is far from an inescapable consequence of his severe learning disability.

Mr A

A care plan for Mr A would look very similar to George's but there would need to be an additional element for his attempts to masturbate in public. Because of his previous long-term institutionalisation it may take a couple of years for the damage done by that service in undermining notions of privacy to be repaired. To keep staff's motivation over such a long period it is worth regularly recording the frequency of public masturbation to mark the improvement.

Sex education

There are a number of ways by which Mr A could be helped to understand that it is good to masturbate in private but not in public. The success of these would very much depend on his communication ability. Possibilities include:

■ showing him images of men masturbating and trying to ensure he associates these with good places to masturbate, for example, putting a line drawing of a man masturbating in his bedroom

■ leading him directly to the bedroom whenever he attempts to masturbate in public

■ when there is a recognition that Mr A has worked out that it is acceptable to masturbate in his bedroom then rather than leading him to the bedroom it may be appropriate to apply minor sanctions when he does lapse back into public masturbation.

See Case checklist J: Care planning

part three

 4 The Response-ability of the Service Network

I n this section, we have looked at the service system and the mechanisms which exist for co-ordinating the different inputs of day and residential services, employment and leisure, specialist and professional expertise: this is what we have termed in the subtitle of this manual the system's *response-ability*.

Suggestions for responses to men with learning disabilities who sexually abuse must be mindful of both the immediate and broader environments where the men live, and the services which the men may access. In many cases the 'solutions' may seem very obvious but it is impractical for these to be realised in the current context of the men's services. For this reason we have included this section, which examines the *ability* of services to respond effectively to the issues presented by abusive sexual behaviour. This is not just a question of financial restraints but is often a factor of the philosophy and organisation of local services.

Which agency is accountable?

Once services accept a responsibility to take appropriate steps to prevent a man with learning disabilities from sexually abusing, they are faced with the need to consider which specific agencies have a share in that responsibility and how their collective efforts are to be co-ordinated. Many of the men have complex service arrangements involving different agencies, including residential, day and leisure services which may be variously managed by private and voluntary organisations, or health and social services departments. In addition they may receive specialist health input including psychology, community nursing or psychiatry.

The mechanics of making these arrangements work is not special to men who sexually abuse; their cases merely point out the extent to which these arrangements can fall down. In our research we found that it was the ordinary co-ordination which failed rather than the specialist input or programmes. In other words, although these men are among the most difficult to work with, it was not the actual complexity of the men's problems or the bleakness of their lives which tested services but the need to get the infrastructure working and the services pulling in the same direction.

We will now take a look at the specific responsibilities of commissioners and providers of services and at how these can be meshed into a coherent response to the man's problems.

Commissioner's accountability

Purchasers of services fall into two categories both of whom have a part to play in the management of services for men with learning disabilities who sexually offend (Flynn & Brown, 1997). At authority level they are responsible for commissioning services across their catchment area to meet the needs of an identified client group. At a more local level individual care managers will make and supervise placements within that service network (Brown, 1996). Their work will usually be organised through local partnership boards.

The distinctions between purchasers and providers of services in the UK were instituted in theory to simplify the lines of accountability for learning disability services. For the majority of men with learning disabilities living in the community, their residential and day services are purchased by social services. Where men receive health-managed residential or day services, the funding arrangements are more complex. Sometimes this may be paid for by social services, sometimes health and sometimes a combination of both. Other potential purchasers of services for men with learning disability are education and probation. A few men may be in receipt of direct payments administered by them with assistance from family members or support workers.

With purchasing of services comes the legal responsibility to ensure that each service is appropriate to the needs of the individual who receives them. To exercise this responsibility, purchasers are required to set up monitoring arrangements. This does not always happen, particularly where placements are made by a number of authorities to services outside their areas – this was reflected in the inquiry into abuse of people with learning disabilities by staff in a private home in Buckinghamshire (Burgner Enquiry into LongCare Ltd, established 1997).

For purchasers to exercise their responsibility with regard to men with learning disabilities who sexually abuse, there is an obligation to ensure that *on entry* to the service there are sufficient grounds to suggest that the service will meet the man's needs. This would include checking out:

■ what access the man will have to vulnerable people

■ the man's own level of safety

■ the service's general level of competence to manage men with learning disabilities who have sexually abused

■ the provisional management plan for the man.

The reality is often very different, with care managers desperate to place such men anywhere, regardless of the placement's suitability in terms of other potentially vulnerable service-users, and/or its competence to address the men's needs. Men are often admitted to institutions or private facilities when their abusive behaviour becomes too much for the local services to contain, but what is being bought is not competency to manage the men's behaviour by the service but a willingness of the service to tolerate it – not that the ensuing victims get any say in this financial arrangement.

Once men with histories of abusing are placed in services the necessary monitoring by the purchaser should include:

■ being informed of any further incidents of abusive behaviour

■ being informed if the man himself is abused

■ being kept up-to-date with care plans

■ regular visits to see the man within the service

■ agreements about psychological input and supervision of care programmes, including the funding arrangements for this

■ regular health checks and reviews of medication with an informed GP who has access to the man's records including any psychiatric history or mental health problems.

A key responsibility for the purchaser is to ensure that the service is equipped with appropriate information about the man's abusive behaviour, because without it the service itself will be unable to identify or implement preventative strategies.

Purchasers are required to keep within budgets and men with sexually abusive behaviours are expensive to serve. This can lead to conflicts of interest which may or may not become explicit. *Providers* need to negotiate a clear mandate when they are considering putting in place additional staffing or supervision of a man deemed to present a risk, but *purchasers* may be tempted to discount their assessment if it involves extra spending. Independent risk management (Churchill *et al*, 1997) may help both parties to make realistic but ethical decisions in such situations. Within the research one case did lead to such a conflict of interest: a social services purchaser was trying to reduce the cost of a service while the provider was trying to get additional funding for supervision of a man following a recent sexual assault on a child. The residential service was in the voluntary sector and had, reasonably, temporarily suspended the man from going out by himself and had called a meeting with social services to discuss his continuing care management. The meeting eventually took place four months after the initial incident when debate about the service's intervention led to a critical response from social services on the grounds that the restriction to the man's movement was an infringement of his rights. Services are damned if they do and damned if they don't in such a situation. They need to be able to get prompt access to negotiate a new mandate when abuse comes to light and to get support for any intervention they institute to protect other service-users and/or prevent further assaults.

Provider accountability

The purchasers share their accountability with any services which the men access. The priority of any service is to ensure that its environment is not conducive to abusive behaviour. It is difficult to argue that services which have institutional models of practice can do anything but turn a blind eye to abuse (Crossmaker, 1991). Services which recognise their deficits in this area should not regard themselves as suitable facilities for men with learning disabilities with histories of sexually abusing, as it is predictable that their behaviour will be allowed to continue with few, if any, checks. Unfortunately, services are rarely this direct with purchasers about their limitations.

For specific men who have sexually abused, it is the responsibility of the provider agency in collaboration with the care manager to identify a care plan which states exactly how the risk of abusing will be managed. The care plan should be made available to the purchaser, who should also be informed when changes to the care plan are being considered. Ideally the care plan should be produced in partnership with the purchaser. The research study found no examples of services working within such contractual agreements – specific care plans which explicitly addressed the sexually abusive behaviour were absent at the beginning and still in the process of being developed at the end of our period of work, which tended to suggest a 'crossed fingers' approach to risk management, rather than considered and proactive planning. Where plans had been written, they were often not actually used and updated. Therefore, in addition to the responsibility of individual services to produce care plans, there is the obvious responsibility to implement them.

Services should recognise that they are in part responsible for the sexually abusive behaviour of men with learning disabilities. They should, therefore, be willing to justify what action they undertake to prevent assaults. Because a whole set of circumstances currently militate against effective service partnerships, it may be necessary for providers to take the initiative in providing significant people with information to help them decide what level of intervention is appropriate in the service network, and to support the mandate for the proposed interventions.

Service structures

In our research we found that the **ability** of individual services to respond effectively to the abusive behaviour of men was dependant on the organisation of the local health and social services. To illustrate this, we have provided two examples which are loosely based on the services we encountered.

Ruralville

Ruralville is a quiet seaside town distant from any major cities. Its population is relatively stable, major changes being young people leaving the area to find work or study, and older people coming to the town as a favoured retirement location. The population of people with learning disabilities is also very stable, having avoided the influx found in other seaside towns from the closure of large institutions and cost-saving placements from large cities.

For a number of years, health and social services have undertaken **joint commissioning** for learning disability services and a good relationship between the two departments has developed. Because there is little change either with the staff who operate services or with the people who use them, there is a sense that the people with learning disabilities and their needs are well known. Further it appears that the services are well matched to address the extent of needs.

Residential and day services are primarily managed by social services, the remainder of services being run by voluntary organisations. There are few private services in the area. Specialist support teams for people with learning disabilities are provided by both health and social services. These include a strong psychology team and a social services outreach team which provides support to people living outside staffed accommodation.

The only weakness in the local service network is the consultant psychiatrist for people with learning disabilities. He has acquired a reputation as being over-enthusiastic in the prescription of medication, to the extent that local workers are reluctant to make referrals to him.

At the time of the research only one out-of-area placement was being funded.

Innerborough

Innerborough is an inner city area which scores highly on all the major indices of social deprivation, including unemployment, overcrowded accommodation, and poor health. There is a culturally diverse population and both health and social services face enormous challenges meeting the ever increasing needs of the local communities, a task which is made more demanding because of language and cultural variations.

Social services has undergone a number of major reorganisations in the last few years, one being to oscillate between generic social workers at neighbourhood offices and specialist, boroughwide teams. At the time of the research, generic care management was in place, with care managers holding cases from a variety of client groups. Services for people with learning disabilities were the responsibility of a principal officer – a position which was vacated soon after the research began; eventually the work was absorbed into the role of another principal officer who had no experience in the area of learning disability.

The health support to people with disabilities included specialised community nurses and a psychologist. These were co-ordinated within one team. The consultant psychiatrist was well integrated into this team which functioned well. However, it faced a high staff turnover which was a feature of all local services – over the course of the research over half of the posts in this team were vacated. There was little history of joint commissioning between health and social services in the area of learning disability, and co-ordination between the two agencies was extremely limited, the problem being compounded by the difficulty in identifying a focal person within social services.

Day services were run by both social services and voluntary organisations. Two of these stood out as particularly bleak in terms of their run-down environments. Social services no longer managed any residential facilities. Instead these were now run largely by voluntary organisations, with health maintaining an adult respite service. There was limited private provision in the area.

In contrast to Ruralville there was little sense of the local services having a good knowledge of the extent of needs of the local population with learning disabilities. The feeling was of an inadequate number of services struggling to cope with the unending demands placed upon them. Another significant difference was the greater reliance of Innerborough on out-of-area placements.

Your own service may share features of both of these. Below we draw out how different service patterns may impact on the ability to respond.

Joint commissioning

Joint commissioning involves local health and social services deciding together how they will meet the needs of people with learning disabilities in the area. Its main commendation is the potential to provide a comprehensive range of services which are well integrated. This system was well represented in Ruralville. Unfortunately, the reverse was true in Innerborough, where it was difficult to find evidence of co-operative work between the two agencies focused on the needs of people with learning disabilities. On a practical level this meant that meetings between the two often involved contesting who should provide or pay for the services for a particular individual.

Without joint commissioning, stretched services reasonably try to limit their responsibilities – those people to whom they do not have a statutory responsibility may be referred on, only to find other doors closed to them. In this way people with learning disabilities can fall through a gap between health and social services.

Out-of-area placements

Out-of-area placements – where people with learning disabilities are funded to receive services in another part of the country – can be viewed in a number of ways. Most positively it can reflect a commitment for the local services to meet people's needs in the most appropriate services regardless of location. For example, Ruralville's one out-of-area placement was for a man to attend at a specialist forensic residential service for people with learning disabilities – a provision which was not locally available. The opposite end of the spectrum is that the extent of out-of-area placements can point to major service deficiencies, including:

■ the willingness to send people away from their home communities with the intention to purchase services at a lower cost than those available locally. This is a real dilemma for many inner-city boroughs where staff and accommodation costs are high compared to other parts of the country

■ a reflection of the local services' inability to meet locally the diverse needs of people with learning disabilities. Innerborough's practice with regard to out-of-area placements was definitely influenced by the availability of lower-cost placements away from the city. The human cost of this is that often people with learning disabilities are moved away from their friends, family and communities.

The risks of out-of-area placements for people with learning disabilities have been highlighted in a series of cases involving poor monitoring arrangements by distant social services departments (ADSS/NAPSAC, 1996).

Knowledge of local needs

The benefits of a good picture of the local needs in the area of learning disability are clear. It allows services to be designed and developed to fit the needs of the local learning disabled population. This matching is helped by the availability of sufficient resources to meet the need; however, even where resources are scarce it allows for greater planning and prioritising of resource allocation.

Relationships between key professionals

Obviously good relationships between professionals both within and across agencies simplify the task of developing consistent service plans which can be successfully implemented. A problem of the generic model of social services in Innerborough was that the very limited contact individual social workers and case managers had with learning disability services gave little opportunity to build and maintain relationships.

In Ruralville, interdisciplinary relationships were generally much stronger than those in Innerborough. The only obvious weakness was the relative professional isolation of the consultant psychiatrist from other health workers, very different to Innerborough where the consultant psychiatrist was part of a well functioning health-based team.

With so many people and agencies involved, it is crucial that someone takes responsibility for co-ordinating the service at individual and agency level. Sometimes the services need to be in a hierarchical relationship to each other and this needs to be spelt out. Partnerships do not flourish where commitments are vague, but do so within clearly defined and specified roles.

For example, we have identified specific areas in this manual where psychological input and assessment are called for, but if a residential service fails to heed their advice, a commissioner could be paying for guidance which is not taken up or implemented. Moreover, professional supervision and risk management in these cases cannot be made to work without a clear understanding of the roles of different professionals. Recourse to mental health assessment and occasionally to detention under the *Mental Health Act 1983* may also be required. Residential workers need to know when they should work within professional guidelines and when they are free to manoeuvre and develop their own solutions. This is best where it works on the basis of collaboration and supportive relationships but, especially when resources are stretched, each part of the service needs to pool what energy and resources they have and not undermine each other, reinvent wheels nor make complex decisions which are outside an individual's area of expertise (Brown & Cambridge, 1995).

activity **3e** Assessing your local services

This list is designed to assess the ability of your local services to respond to men with learning disabilities who have unacceptable or abusive sexual behaviour. The more questions you are able to tick, the greater the possibility of a coherent response.

Is there joint commissioning between health and social services? ☐

Is case management by social services in place and effective at co-ordinating the service of an individual with learning disabilities? ☐

Do social services provide specialist case managers for people with learning disabilities? ☐

Do health and social services have a good understanding of the extent of local need? ☐

Do good relationships exist between key people responsible for learning disability services? ☐

Do forums exist which bring different services together to share experiences and to plan future initiatives? ☐

part three

5 Ethical Perspectives

Working with men with learning disabilities who have histories of sexually abusing raises many ethical challenges. These largely concern the tensions between acting in the man's best interests, respecting his rights and protecting potential victims. At times it may be possible to satisfy all of these criteria simultaneously, but generally services will have to make a choice about which factors will be privileged to the detriment of others. Unfortunately services are rarely conscious of the ethical compromises they are making when they respond to men with learning disabilities who have sexually abused. The aim of this section is to illustrate these ethical debates and to provide a framework for multi-disciplinary decision making.

---

activity 3.f Finding the balance

Andrew

Andrew had committed a number of incidents of exposure to local children around the group home where he lived. The parents on each occasion did not want charges to be made. The staff tried to minimise the risk by operating a high level of informal supervision and requesting that he did not go out without staff. Unfortunately, Andrew was not compliant with this regime and he managed to commit a further offence. The staff recognised that they could not guarantee an adequate level of safety for the children in the locality, and reluctantly agreed that he should move to an isolated institution where it would be easier to control the risk to children. They openly acknowledged that this was not in Andrew's best interests, because his personal development, which they had worked hard to support, would suffer greatly within the institution.

continued...

William

William's history of sexual assaults against less able people in the institution where he used to live had resulted in him being prescribed medication which was intended to be a sexual suppressant. He remained on this drug after he moved to the community. Staff there were concerned about the side effects, in particular how his breasts had developed, and raised the subject with his GP who said it would be at their risk if the medication was withdrawn. Staff were also worried it might affect any sexual contact he might have with his current girlfriend who was unaware of his abusive past.

Graham

A woman with learning disabilities whose breast had been grabbed at the day centre by Graham was very upset by the incident. Her key worker at the residential unit argued that it was not right that she should be expected to continue going to the day service with him, and tried to persuade the centre to exclude Graham indefinitely. This was unsuccessful and all that was achieved was a verbal commitment that he would be watched more carefully.

Siad

Siad had caused considerable problems because of his staring at women and children when he went out alone to the local shops. The most recent incident involved him following two young boys into the park. There had been no sexual contact but the boys had been worried enough about the incident to tell their parents who demanded that Siad was not to be allowed out by himself again. Although there had not been one recorded incident of indecent assault in Siad's past, staff were very worried about how the local community might react if they saw him out alone, particularly since there had already been a lot of resistance to the group home. As a consequence they instructed Siad to stay in unless there was a staff member who could escort him. Siad was not happy about this but was compliant with the instruction.

■ What ethical dilemmas were faced in each of the above situations?

■ What decisions would you have made and why?

Competing principles

The following pages will outline some of the ethical decisions which arise when working with men with learning disabilities who sexually abuse, some of which are illustrated in **Activity 3f**. Rather than seeking to provide an answer to the various moral questions, we seek to chart the territory which should be explored when considering individual situations. A number of competing principles come into play in the decisions which you have been considering throughout this manual. These include:

- individual rights

- autonomy vs protection

- best interests

- needs of victims

- parity

- rationing of resources.

Individual rights

Since the *Human Rights Act* was introduced in the UK, we all have certain rights as citizens and this extends to men with learning disabilities who are suspected of sexually abusing. Some rights are mandatory if the man has contact with the criminal justice system, for example:

- the right to a fair trial

- the right to have a solicitor

- specific to having a learning disability, the right to have the support of an 'appropriate adult', but as has been shown earlier, the legal system is not well equipped to cope with people with learning disabilities.

In 1998, human rights set out in the European Convention of Human Rights were enshrined in English law. These include the right to life, the prohibition of torture, slavery and forced labour, the right to liberty and security, to a fair trial and no punishment without legal safeguards; to privacy and family life, freedom of thought, conscience and religion, freedom of expression and association and the right to marry and start a family. Rights to education, to own property, vote in free elections and to be free from discrimination are also assured. Where these rights seem to be in conflict, the right to life and to protection from torture or degrading treatment will always take precedence over the right to privacy and family life. Security is paramount. Any infringement of one right in the interest of another should be proportionate.

Autonomy vs protection

People may name other rights, for example, the right to confidentiality, to freedom of movement, to refuse medical intervention, but these are not absolutes, particularly when the citizens are people with learning disabilities whose cognitive abilities may undermine their desirability. For example, few would argue for total freedom of movement for a person with learning disabilities who lacked the road skills necessary to be reasonably safe near traffic, but the moral complexity of limiting a person with learning disabilities' movements without a specific legal mandate is huge, and recently led to a legal challenge in Strasbourg (Bournewood).

Both Siad and Andrew (see **Activity 3f**, pages 163–164) faced restrictions on their movement because of their behaviour, and this is likely to be what the local community would have wanted. However, it is important to recognise that no other man whose case had not been processed through the criminal justice system would be expected to tolerate such a limit to his freedom. Staff may present this as a 'choice' for the men concerned as a way of satisfying their own ethical ambiguities over their action, but this is a false argument because one needs to acknowledge the extent of the influence of staff in making a decision which no one else would reasonably adhere to. Andrew's unwillingness to comply with his 'house arrest' demonstrates clearly that staying with staff was not his choice. What staff are really doing is advising or telling the men what to do. They can powerfully control the movements of some people because of their histories of compliance with staff requests.

These attempts to restrict the men's movements may still be ethically justifiable within learning disability services. In fact, a failure to do so could reasonably result in legal action being taken against the responsible authority. For example, it would be difficult to argue that a service was exercising its duty of care if a woman with poor road skills was found wandering alone in town. From a different angle there is a growing consensus that the rights of men who have committed sexual offences should be restricted beyond the course of any prison sentence they serve, for example Schedule 1 offenders are uniquely required to report their residence to the police.

But there are contradictions in relying on the learnt compliance of men with learning disabilities to guard against future incidents of abuse. This is because the men's behaviour could be related to their experience of disempowerment which may very well be reinforced by such interventions. However, this may be a necessary and pragmatic strategy which best serves the interests of the men.

Best interests

Instead of focusing entirely on upholding the apparent rights of men with learning disabilities, services may seek to make ethical decisions guided by the man's best interests. This is by no means straightforward because different parties including the man himself will have differing views on what is in fact in the man's best interest. For example, both Siad and Andrew may believe it is in their best interests to go out by themselves whilst staff may believe it is in the men's best interests for them to be escorted out by staff. The research itself highlighted another contradiction: in seeking the men's consent to participate, the men were theoretically making a choice that it was in their interest to do so. However, there is a long recognised pattern of men with learning disabilities getting away with their abusive behaviour (see for example, Hayes, 1991), a pattern which may have been called into question by the research. Informed services may believe that they should directly address the men's behaviour but it is understandable that some men with learning disabilities would be resistant to this. Moreover the men may be more at risk from 'nice' informal interventions than they are within the formal structures of the criminal justice and mental health systems which have safeguards built into them, especially for people without the capacity to make their own decisions or whose cognitive skills render them vulnerable. In future, it is likely that the Court of Protection, acting under the mental capacity legislation, will be the final arbiter of these decisions.

The ambiguity of 'best interest' should always be recognised, not least because the consequences of any intervention may not be anticipated. For example, one man in the research study disclosed his own experience of abuse which was confirmed by an independent investigation. However, the emotional cost to him of the process of the investigation raised questions about whether his involvement really could be understood as in his best interests. Another example was where direct work with a man with learning disabilities revealed much more than was previously known about his history of sexually abusing. The report was then subsequently used to support his detention under the *Mental Health Act 1983*, even though such action was believed to be unnecessary and contrary to the man's long-term needs by the author of that report.

Needs of victims

It can be strongly argued that the men's best interests or rights should not take precedence over the needs of victims or potential victims. So perhaps Noah (see **Activity 3a**, page 99) should not have his past withheld from his girlfriend or her supporters, and maybe Graham should be excluded indefinitely from the day centre (see **Activity 3f**, pages 163–164). Similarly, the attempts to restrict both Siad's and Andrew's movements will have arisen out of a concern to prevent further abuse (see **Activity 3f**).

The attention given to the sexual abuse of people with learning disabilities has strengthened these arguments greatly, so that people are now asserting that a woman with learning disabilities should not have to continue to live with a man who had assaulted or raped her, nor is it acceptable for men with histories of sexually abusing to share services with particularly vulnerable adults (McCarthy & Thompson, 1996). Unfortunately these ideas are not common currency in many services, and decisions about the management of men with learning disabilities who sexually abuse are often divorced from the risk that is posed to other people, most notably other people with learning disabilities. In our case studies, note that it was the men who posed a risk to people **outside services** in the local community who experienced the greatest restrictions to their freedom in an attempt to control their behaviour. This is a reflection of the fact that responses to men with learning disabilities who sexually abuse are determined more by who the victim is than the seriousness of the assault (Thompson, 1997b).

The victim perspective does not itself provide a complete framework for making ethical decisions about the management of men with learning disabilities who sexually abuse. For example, is it necessarily the case that Graham should be excluded indefinitely from the day service for grabbing the woman's breast (see **Activity 3f**, pages 163–164)? Should his degree of learning disability, the availability of other services and the benefits of the current day service for him be allowed to influence this decision? It may be that different forms of abuse between service-users are commonplace within the service, for example, violence that is termed 'challenging behaviour'. If this is the case, is it fair to exclude Graham for a single incident of sexual violence? This gives rise to a fourth framework for arriving at ethical decisions, that of fairness or equitable access to resources. Proportionality is also an important value to consider in this kind of situation.

Parity

Another approach to resolving the conflicting interests of victims and perpetrators is to seek responses which are comparable with those received by other perpetrator groups for similar sexual offences, or by other men with learning disabilities for different forms of violence. This is not to suggest that these other responses are necessarily ideal, but parity provides a reference point which is often lacking. At different times men with learning disabilities who sexually abuse are treated both more harshly and less harshly than abusers who do not have learning disabilities. For example, it has been found that men with learning disabilities who have been sectioned as an outcome of their sexual crimes are being kept in institutions longer than men with mental health problems detained for more serious sexual assaults (Murrey, Briggs & Davis, 1992). Conversely, men like Graham (see **Activity 3f**) and Malcolm (see **Activity 3a**) are regularly getting away with their assaults against other people with learning disabilities and women staff.

A framework of parity therefore provides a scale against which responses to men with learning disabilities can be judged. From this context it seems reasonable for staff to restrict Andrew's (see **Activity 3f**) movements for exposing himself to children as other men could receive a custodial sentence for such offences. In contrast, it is very unlikely that any man would be sent to prison for simply staring at children as is the case with Siad (see **Activity 3f**). Returning to Graham, it would appear unreasonable to single out his sexual assault against a woman at the day centre as a reason for indefinite exclusion if violent assaults are frequent in the centre and do not receive responses of this magnitude.

Rationing of resources

The availability of resources is inevitably going to affect ethical decisions about what happens to men with learning disabilities who sexually abuse. Potentially this may override all the criteria highlighted above. It could have been the case that the staffing structures in Siad's and Andrew's home would not have allowed the level of supervision that was recommended. It is also the case that requests to social services for additional staffing in such situations are not always met. For example, when John, another man we met, committed a serious assault against a woman he shared the house with, the service responded by paying for additional staffing so that he could be watched more carefully. Although this was not necessarily the most useful action which could have been taken, failing on both criteria of parity and the needs of the victims, it did have enormous resource implications. Several months later, social services were keen to reduce their financial commitment although there was no indication to suggest that the risk to the woman was any less.

The availability of resources could also have affected the decision not to exclude Graham (see **Activity 3f**) from the day centre: it would have been a lot more difficult to do so if there was no other suitable service for him locally. Definitely one reason why John (above) was not moved after sexually assaulting the woman he lived with was the difficulty of finding another placement.

Malcolm's case (see **Activity 3a**) points to other resource issues which rarely gain attention. The pattern of a man entering learning disability services for the first time after he has committed a sexual offence is not uncommon in both community and institutional settings. The question of whether this man does have *learning disabilities* has to be asked. He clearly has *needs* but does this mean that they are necessarily best met within learning disability services, using precious learning disability resources? Typically, when these questions are addressed to service providers they are answered with the statement that no other service will work with the man. The inherent contradiction in this reply is not recognised: although the boundaries which other services put around themselves are respected, it seems that learning disability services are not allowed to assert their own boundaries. This gives rise to an expanding and flexible definition of learning disabilities and an even greater pressure on resources. Further, as is common, Malcolm being very able and new to the service, gains privileged access to these resources as is demonstrated by the attention of the psychologist. The price of this response to Malcolm's behaviour will be indirectly felt by other people with learning disabilities, most notably less able and less challenging individuals who will have to share further stretched resources. It was also felt more directly by the vulnerable women he exploited, to whom he was given easy and unchecked access.

The attention which has brought men with learning disabilities who sexually abuse into focus has meant that services may now be more willing to commit extra resources to support them. Again, because resources are finite, it is important to question the value of any input which is provided and whether evolving spending priorities best serve the interests of people with learning disabilities generally rather than a few individuals. One psychotherapeutic service for people with learning disabilities which was originally focused on working with people with learning disabilities who have been sexually abused, has seen an enormous shift towards referrals for men with learning disabilities who have sexually abused others. One reading of this is that services are more willing to pay for psychotherapy for men who abuse than for clients who have been abused. Particularly since psychotherapy, like any other treatment, has yet to demonstrate its true effectiveness, there needs to be a discussion of its costs and benefits which includes the possibility that there may be a knock-on effect of compromise for the treatment to victims of abuse.

An ethical framework for responding

It should be recognised that those people working with a man who has sexually abused are not always best placed to make ethical decisions about what action should be taken. In some ways it is inevitable that contact with the man will lead to a loss of objectivity and a desire to limit the consequences for him. Therapists who work with men without learning disabilities who sexually abuse acknowledge this and try to limit it through supervision. This tendency was illustrated at a case conference shortly after one of Andrew's (see **Activity 3f**) early assaults against a child. At the end he asked whether it was still all right for him to go on holiday the following week. Because the situation was so painful for him and staff, the desire to make it better was so strong that no one raised any objection to this. It was left to someone who had not had previous contact with Andrew to point out how unhelpful this would be in trying to make sure he understood the seriousness of his behaviour, a viewpoint which, once articulated, was supported by the meeting as a whole.

See Case checklist K: Ethics ▶▶

The ethical dilemmas in responding to men with learning disabilities are too complicated to be reduced to a prescriptive list of priorities. Instead **Case checklist K: Ethics** is offered as a set of questions which should be asked when making care planning decisions.

Service networks cannot get it right all the time. What matters is that decisions are made openly and that as many viewpoints as possible are heard. Some counties have ethical review committees to refer to for such considerations.

In England and Wales the absence of a legal framework for decision making with, and on behalf of, people who are unable to take specific decisions for themselves has recently been addressed. This should help protect both men with learning disabilities and their potential victims from the informality, inconsistency and lack of accountability of decision making which this study found.

The central principles of the new legislation are to support people wherever possible to make their own decisions, and where this is not possible to make decisions based on the best interests of the person concerned.

The *Adults with Incapacity (Scotland) Act 2000* now allows application to the local Sheriff for a Guardianship Order to make specific decisions on behalf of another person. In England and Wales, the *Mental Capacity Act 2005* introduces changes to the Court of Protection so that complex welfare decisions can be referred to it alongside financial and medical matters. This Court also has the power to appoint deputies who will have enduring decision-making powers. Now that formal authority for decision making on behalf of others is available it is important that men with learning disabilities who sexually abuse are given the protection this is intended to provide. Therefore these decisions should be referred to either the local Sheriff or Court of Protection – options which were not available when this study took place.

Regardless of whether there is formal decision-making authority, discussions of best interests should involve a variety of individuals with different experiences. Social services as the purchasing authority should be central to these discussions. After all, if they do not fundamentally agree to the decisions an individual service makes, they would be contradicting themselves by lending support through their continuing purchase of the service. For example, when Andrew's (see **Activity 3f** on page 163) staff explained to social services that they were not letting Andrew go out by himself because of the fear of further incidents, the purchaser disputed the decision, citing Andrew's right to freedom. They did not, however, present any other suggestions, demand that Andrew should be allowed out, or threaten to withdraw funding and therefore were, by default, condoning but failing to support the provider agency's actions.

Because these ethical decisions are so difficult and can impact greatly on the lives of the men with learning disabilities concerned and their victims, a minimal standard is to record what action is being taken and why.

Prevention

This manual has concerned itself with recognising and responding to men with learning disabilities who sexually abuse. A good response will minimise the risk of the man re-offending and so prevent further abuse. This is just one side of prevention. The other is for services to be alert to the possibility of men abusing and to be strategic about taking action which will limit its occurrence. In **Part Three** we have set out some of the local service arrangements which are themselves key building blocks in providing safer services (see **Activity 3e** on page 162). In addition to these, we would add the following as specific indicators of services which have taken a proactive approach to the risks of sexually abusing.[1] You may want to think about your own service and decide in what areas it is doing well and what are the priorities for improvement.

Policies

- Policies which respect the right of people with learning disabilities to enjoy consented sexual relationships.

- Policies which address the potential for people with learning disabilities to be abused and to abuse.

- Guidelines which set out thresholds and referral routes within local multi-agency adult protection procedures.

Service-user education

- Advocacy and self-advocacy arrangements to ensure services are accountable and are delivered to meet users' needs.

- Sex education and assertiveness courses for service-users.

Staff training

- Staff are trained and supported to treat people with respect.

- All staff are trained to recognise abuse and to know how to respond if abuse is suspected.

- High recognition of the need for gender-specific services, so that at times it will be important to provide staff of a particular gender; for example, male staff to work with men who persistently abuse women staff.

---

1 These are similar to those suggested for preventing the sexual abuse of people with learning disabilities in McCarthy & Thompson (1996).

Service management and design

■ Service environments that offer people dignity; for example, quality, well-kept buildings.

■ Services provided to meet individual service-user needs rather than service-users fitted into inflexible services.

■ Careful attention to the risks and benefits of people with learning disabilities sharing services with other people.

Commissioning

■ Availability of men-only residential services for men who pose a persistent risk of abuse to women service-users or staff.

■ Availability of women-only services for women who are particularly vulnerable to abuse.

■ Local capacity for people to be moved immediately (residential and day services); for example, to separate an abuser from his victim.

Legal

■ Trained appropriate adults available 24 hours a day.

■ Co-operative liaison with the local police.

■ Knowledge and use of formal decision-making processes.

Conclusion

We hope that this workbook has helped you and your service to make confident and clear decisions on behalf of the men you are working with and those who are affected by their behaviour. It is inevitable that such decisions are complex and uncomfortable but it is important that you do reach consensus and draw up shared plans. A few years ago there was a popular dictum 'not to decide is a decision'. We have taken a stand against 'not deciding' in this manual which we hope you share. We believe that 'not deciding' is a decision not to support these men, many of whom have had difficult lives and who are almost uniquely disadvantaged and stigmatised both within services and within their local communities. We are committed to developing response-ability since the only alternative is to turn away.

Photocopiable Resources

Activities

Activity 1a: How good is your information?

Activity 1b: Where do you stand?

Activity 1c: Acceptable, unacceptable, inappropriate or abusive?

Activity 1d: Abusive or unacceptable?

Activity 1e: Sorting out consent issues to clarify abuse

Activity 1f: Private behaviours

Activity 2a: Understanding the men's behaviour

Activity 2b: Mr B

Activity 2c: Problems with masturbation

Activity 2d: Sexual interest in children

Activity 2e: Harassing women staff

Activity 3a: Service responsibility

Activity 3b: Information management

Activity 3c: Sharing information

Activity 3d: Sharing information – 'Need to Know'

Activity 3e: Assessing your local services

Activity 3f: Finding the balance

activity

1a | How good is your information?

In your organisation:

1 Are staff:

- ▓ negative about *all* sexual contacts including consenting sexual relationships (opposite-sex and same-sex) between people with learning disabilities?

- ▓ *laissez-faire* in their attitudes so that unconsenting sex may be wrongly interpreted as mutual, or as a relationship?

- ▓ careful to distinguish consented from unconsented sex, and mindful of the vulnerability of people with learning disabilities to exploitation?

2 Do clients have 'reputations' which are not supported by documentation?

3 Have past incidents of abuse (or possible abuse) been left unrecorded because:

- ▓ abuse would not have been recognised?

- ▓ no sexual matters were recorded on people's files?

- ▓ the service may have tried to cover up what happened in some way?

- ▓ the service was unwilling to record anything which could not be definitely proved?

4 Do individuals and/or organisations use 'confidentiality' as an excuse not to pass on important information about clients you have responsibility for?

activity

1b Where do you stand?

This exercise works best in a group as it generates lively discussions about people's values and how they have reached their particular point of view. If you are reading the book on your own you can think about where you stand in relation to each statement and perhaps think of the different influences which have led to your views.

Place four large sheets of flip chart paper in the four corners of the room with the following headings on them:

■ **Agree**

■ **Agree with reservations**

■ **Disagree**

■ **Disagree with reservations**

You can put a fifth heading in the middle of the room saying **'Don't know'** or **'On the fence'**.

Then read out one of the statements below and ask each person in your group to stand by the heading which most sums up their view. When they have taken up a position, ask them to look around and find someone with similar views to talk to – give them five minutes to explore why they arrived at the same place. Then ask them to find someone with different views (standing in a different position) and talk to them about why they think as they do. This will allow group members to think about their own, and other people's, views.

You will see that the statements are ambiguous and that group members may respond on the basis of:

■ their own views and personal/religious values

■ their views about what is 'normal' and/or 'typical'

■ what is meant by certain words and terms.

Allow people to explore all of these dimensions and reflect these issues back to them as a dilemma and source of confusion. After all, that is the force field within which a staff group has to make its judgements.

Allow ten minutes per item; if you have limited time, select which items you think are useful in your particular service or setting.

continued...

activity

Where do you stand? (continued)

The statements

- Whatever consenting adults do in private is their own affair.

- Some degree of violence is acceptable in male-female relationships.

- It is not unusual for women to get hurt during sex.

- Anal sex is quite rightly forbidden in lots of religions.

- Men with learning disabilities should be stopped from doing things which might stigmatise them further.

- Men with learning disabilities should have the same rights as other men when it comes to sexual matters.

- Pornography increases the incidence of sexual attacks and abuse.

- Pornography provides a safe outlet for men who cannot find willing partners.

You can add statements if there are particular issues which your staff team is concerned about.

activity

1c | Acceptable, unacceptable, inappropriate or abusive?

The following scenarios are designed to help you think about boundaries and imagine how, as a staff team, you can reach consistent and respectful judgements. In each case think about how you would describe the man's sexual behaviour – would you describe it as acceptable, unacceptable, inappropriate or abusive and on what basis would you decide? What are your principles when it comes to deciding which sexual behaviours are OK and can be supported?

Peter

Peter is a man with severe learning disabilities who is regularly found trying to masturbate himself. This can happen anywhere, and staff believe it is because he gets bored. When he masturbates he does not try to involve anyone else – it appears that he just does not understand conventions of privacy very well. When Marie sees Peter trying to masturbate she gently directs him to somewhere private. She remembers having been very shocked to see him do this when she first started working with him, but did not mention it to anyone then.

Keith

Keith is a man with severe learning disabilities who needs help in the bathroom. On a number of occasions he has grabbed the breasts of women staff whilst they were supporting him with his intimate care. New staff are particularly vulnerable to these assaults. There are no similar problems when intimate care is provided by men.

Philip

Philip is very able. In his bedroom he keeps a range of pornography which he has acquired himself over the years. He seems very inquisitive about sex and is often asking the women staff questions which they believe they should answer. However sometimes these questions are very personal, for example 'do you have sex with your boyfriend?' Some staff choose to answer these questions honestly whilst others reply that this is a private matter. One senior member of staff got very angry when he asked about her boyfriend and since that time he has avoided asking her about sex.

Roger

Roger was reported as having been seen masturbating in the bushes of a park by a woman who was passing by. The woman had guessed he came from the local learning disability hostel where she had worked a number of years ago and felt staff should be warned about what he was doing because she believed he might get into serious trouble if someone else saw him.

---

activity

1d Abusive or unacceptable?

*Look at the five **Central Case Studies** and use this model to decide whether you think their behaviour is abusive.*

Case study	Abusive intent?	Experienced as abusive?	Do you think it was abusive or unacceptable?
Mr A	☐	☐	
Mr B	☐	☐	
Mr C	☐	☐	
Mr D	☐	☐	
Mr E	☐	☐	

activity

1e Sorting out consent issues to clarify abuse

Read the following case studies and decide which describe(s) the sexual abuse of a person with learning disabilities?

Do you agree with the staff actions in each of these cases?

Ian and Neil

Staff are surprised to hear some noise in Ian's bedroom. They go in and are shocked to find Ian involved in some sexual contact with Neil who is 17. They have been living together in the group home for over a year and are thought to generally get on well together. Ian is 29 and the staff tell him he should not be having sex with such a young man.

Michael and Sheila

Michael is found in a quiet corner of a day centre intimately touching Sheila, a less able woman with learning disabilities. She seems comfortable with the contact and is known to regularly seek Michael's attention at the centre which is the only place they meet. The staff's response is to regret that they do not have access to more private space to allow them to enjoy a more satisfying sexual relationship. They choose not to involve Sheila's parents with whom she lives as they believe they would oppose the relationship.

Amir and Billy

Amir and Billy were found sharing a toilet cubicle by staff at a social club for people with learning disabilities. Staff interviewed them alone about what was happening. Whilst Amir says nothing, Billy complains that he did not like Amir touching his 'privates'. In response they reprimand Amir and closely supervise him whilst he is at the club.

Penny

In a sex education group, Penny reveals that her boyfriend, who also has learning disabilities, has sex with her in the grounds of the hospital in which they both live. She says she likes him a lot but that the sex hurts. The group worker is not surprised because she knows that women with learning disabilities often experience sex as painful (McCarthy, 1993) and keeps this information confidential because she considers it to be a very private matter between Penny and her boyfriend.

---

continued...

Sorting out consent issues to clarify abuse (continued)

Comments on Activity 1.5: Sorting out consent issues to clarify abuse

In some ways it can be argued that by seeking Michael out at the day centre, Sheila was taking some initiative for the sexual contacts she had with him but this does not equate to her giving informed consent to sex. It can be regarded more positively than if it was always Michael who went in search of Sheila.

The staff person who found Neil in Ian's bedroom was initially concerned about whether Neil was being exploited. However, the fact that the contact took place in Ian's bedroom is significant. They should have asked 'how did Neil get to be in Ian's bedroom? Was he in fact taking some initiative for the contact?' Usually when men with learning disabilities take advantage of more vulnerable people they invade their personal space, for example, by bursting into their bedroom, getting into their bed, or following them into the bathroom.

Similarly, before the staff reprimanded Amir for assaulting Billy they needed to question how he was able to get Billy into the toilet cubicle. If there was no evidence of force, intimidation or learnt compliance, it was reasonable to assume that on some level Billy accepted the contact. The complaint only arose as a result of their being 'caught'.

---

activity

1f Private behaviours

Bill

Bill is a man with severe learning disabilities who is regularly found trying to masturbate himself. This can happen anywhere, and staff believe it is because he gets bored. When he masturbates he does not try to involve anyone else – it appears that he just does not understand the conventions of privacy very well. From time to time staff have tried without success to encourage him to masturbate in a toilet cubicle (they do not suggest his bedroom because it is shared). Now they tend to leave him unless he is outside of his home.

Simon

Simon has always seemed interested in children and collects pictures of them from magazines, picture books and comics which he keeps in a scrap book in his room. Individual work with him revealed that he fantasised about having sex with children and used these pictures to masturbate when he was in his bedroom. This raised great anxiety amongst the staff team although there was no indication that he had ever actually done anything untoward with a child. In response staff took away all of his pictures of children and tried to stop him collecting any more.

Arthur

When cleaning Arthur's room staff found a small collection of women's underwear which had obviously been heavily worn by him. They could not work out where he had acquired them – he did not have the skills to buy them from a shop and he would not say anything when they asked him about them. For so called 'hygienic' reasons they threw them away, without telling him.

Paul

Paul is known to play with his faeces when he is in the toilet. This has happened for many years and no one is sure why he does it – he says he gets 'a nice feeling'. Staff have continually tried in different ways to discourage him from this habit. The current strategy is to heavily prompt him to do the clearing up which is necessary after his activities.

Ivan

Ivan has severe learning disabilities. He tries to find objects to stick up his rectum when he is alone in his bedroom. The staff worry about what damage he may do to himself, and are very careful not to leave likely objects lying around and to check his bedroom at night times. However this is an uphill struggle and most mornings there is evidence that he has used something – often pens, pencils or cutlery.

continued...

activity

 1f   **Private behaviours (continued)**

■ Which of the above sexual behaviours would be regarded as unacceptable in your service?

■ Do you agree with this definition?

■ Do you agree with the actions staff have taken in each case?

activity

2a Understanding the men's behaviour

In your group, ask everyone to brainstorm all the factors/explanations they have for sexually abusive behaviour in general. Write up the actual words people use and try to group together those explanations which are to do with:

■ **the individual** who is abusing

■ **their past** (especially previous abuse they might have suffered themselves)

■ **their living conditions**, for example, unemployment or loneliness; as well as

■ more general factors like **society's attitudes** towards women or family break-up.

Do not miss out things which do not fit neatly under one of these headings – some explanations will overlap.

When you have finished look at the whole picture together as if related to a particular man you are working with. Underline or put a circle around those factors which you think are particularly relevant to him and his circumstances. As well as inviting your group to think very broadly about the causes of difficult sexual behaviour, this may also be a useful way of gathering together different kinds of information which is held by different people.

activity

2b Mr B

Mr B

Mr B lived with his mother until he was found in their flat one day with her dead body – the flat was in a disgusting condition with faeces spread all around the rooms. He had not had contact with services before then and neighbours at this time reported that he used to roam markets with his mother collecting food discarded by vendors. At that point he entered learning disability services and was moved to a local hostel. This was ten years ago when he weighed just forty-five kilograms (seven stones). At the hostel they had several problems with his sexual behaviour, including him stripping naked by a window, gesturing masturbation to the neighbours, smearing faeces and urinating in public. The most serious incident occurred shortly after he arrived at the hostel when he started to take his penis out in public and thrust himself against a girl of 12 who was passing. For a while after this incident it was decided that Mr B should not go out unaccompanied. This arrangement had lapsed by the time he moved to a nearby group home when the hostel closed three years ago. He has been diagnosed by a psychiatrist as having hypomania and two years ago spent a short period in a psychiatric hospital which he did not enjoy. His physical condition is very much improved and he is no longer underweight.

The group home attempted to make links with his family and found his brother who showed no interest in re-establishing a relationship. Mr B had a couple of good friends at the hostel but they moved to other areas when it was closed down and he has not had any contact with them since that time. Otherwise the only people he names as important to him are the current staff of the group home. He still thinks a lot about his mother and the neighbourhood in which they used to live together.

In a case conference which followed the assault, Mr B asked if he would still be able to go on a scheduled social outing the following week.

What would your response be?

activity

2c Problems with masturbation

Consider the scenarios below and try to decide how relevant the problems with masturbation are to the men's unacceptable and abusive sexual behaviours.

Mark

Mark has been taking medication for his epilepsy for a number of years. Staff who work with him report that they have never seen him with an erection or trying to play with his penis in any way. They are experiencing major difficulties when women staff are involved in his intimate care: he attempts to grab their breasts when they are helping him. These assaults often cause both pain and embarrassment to the women concerned.

Lloyd

Lloyd spends a lot of time masturbating, both in public and private but no one knows if he ever reaches orgasm. Sometimes when he tries to masturbate he becomes increasingly agitated and reacts quite violently when staff try to intervene to stop him doing it in public or to lead him somewhere more appropriate. Staff have been recording his episodes of violence for some time and have found that the vast majority of them occur when he is interrupted in the course of masturbating.

Matt

Matt has Down's Syndrome and though his parents know he plays with his penis, they have never seen any sign of ejaculation. There is no record of there being a problem with him exposing himself or trying to masturbate in public but at the day centre he regularly goes up to people, especially staff and less able people, and rubs his groin against them. This is assumed to be a sexually motivated act.

---

activity

2d Sexual interest in children

The following scenarios demonstrate what can happen when men with learning disabilities are identified as having a specific sexual interest in children.

Ronnie

Ronnie, a man with mild learning disabilities had invited a young boy of ten whom he met at the park into the flat where he lived by himself with minimal support. Once he was there he tried to have sex with the boy who resisted and then got away. The boy reported what had happened through his parents to the police. As a result, the man was detained temporarily under the Mental Health Act in a learning disability hospital. During this time an assessment revealed that he had a specific sexual interest in pre-pubescent boys. This single piece of information led to the man being moved to a more secure institution where he was to be held indefinitely. This move took place without even consulting the person who had made the assessment about what might be an appropriate service plan.

Greg

Greg was in his 60s and in addition to a mild learning disability, had increasing problems of mobility which meant that he was unable to walk more than a few metres without the support of workers. Whilst in transition from the institution where he had lived for many years to a staffed group home in the community, attention was focused on him talking about wanting young girls to be his girlfriends – these were children he saw in pictures or the staff's own children. An assessment showed that his interest in young girls was not a misunderstanding about appropriate ages for partners but that he was quite clear that he would like to touch them sexually – being particularly interested in their lack of pubic hair. Although there was no knowledge of Greg ever having sexually assaulted a child it was recommended that the group home should exercise some caution when children were around. However, the outcome of this discussion was that the place at the group home was withdrawn as a result of the staff's reaction to his sexual interest in children.

Do you think the outcomes of these situations were appropriate?

activity

2e Harassing women staff

Consider the following two situations – in both cases the men were known to be sexually harassing women staff, including asking them to have sex with them and on occasion trying to grab at their breasts.

Martin

Martin's brother reported that he was worried about Martin's use of pornography. At home Martin spent a lot of time in his room looking at pornography showing women. This could be magazines or videos but recently he was almost continually viewing the pornography station on cable television. His brother had asked the social worker's advice as to whether he should limit Martin's use in any way, in particular to stop the subscription to the cable station. Staff agreed that this would be a useful start.

Chris

When out with a male member of staff from the day service, Chris indicated that he wanted to buy a Playboy style magazine from a newsagent. The staff member accepted this but was concerned about the reaction of his mother if Chris brought it home. Because of this it was suggested to Chris that it was kept safe in the office but that he could ask for it while at the centre to take it somewhere private. The staff's view was that Chris's sexuality was being unfairly denied by his family, and that this was part of the problem in his current abusive behaviour towards women staff.

Do you agree with the staff's suggestions in these cases?

activity

3a Service responsibility

Read the following case studies and think about how responsible Gregory, Noah, Nick and Malcolm are and what responsibility should have been taken by their respective services:

Gregory

Gregory has a history of sexually harassing both women with learning disabilities and women staff. Staff at his group home think that his social isolation might be a contributory factor. In response to this they make arrangements for him to attend a social club for people with learning disabilities. No one at the club is told about his history. On the second occasion he attends, two women with learning disabilities who are regular participants are absent. A phone enquiry reveals that they are avoiding Gregory because he had said some rude things to them the week before.

Noah

Within a large institution, Noah had gained a reputation for sexually exploiting less able people, who were often scared of what he might do if they tried to resist. Since he moved out of the hospital Noah has developed a relationship with a woman at the day centre. The staff who work with him are supportive of the relationship and are making arrangements for the two to have private time together. They have decided to keep his history confidential from the woman and her carers as they believe he should be given a fresh start now he is living in the community. One day his girlfriend complains that he forced her to have sex even though she was clear she did not want to.

Nick

Nick is a man with severe learning disabilities who needs help in the bathroom. On a number of occasions he had grabbed the breasts of women staff whilst they were supporting him with his intimate care. New staff are particularly vulnerable to these assaults. There are no similar problems when intimate care is provided by a man.

---

continued...

activity

3a   Service responsibility (continued)

Malcolm

Malcolm, an unemployed man, had grabbed a woman's breast at a local shopping centre. The police who apprehended him did not believe it was serious enough to press charges but referred him to social services because they thought he may have some sort of learning disability. Although Malcolm had not had any previous contact with learning disability services and seemed to cope with the practicalities of life with a little support from his family, it was suggested that he attends a day service for people with learning disabilities and that he receives individual counselling from the psychologist attached to the unit. Shortly after his arrival at the service, he was found to have taken sexual advantage of a number of less able and unassertive women with learning disabilities who use the service.

■ Are the men fully responsible for these assaults?

■ Are there things the service should have done to prevent the abuse?

activity

3b Information management

Liam

At an assessment meeting staff told the psychologist that, on a number of occasions, a staff member who had since left found Liam in a compromising position with other men at the day centre. Staff were very anxious that he received some form of sexual counselling to stop this. An examination of the case files could not clarify or confirm these incidents. Nor did it seem that any action had been taken against Liam or any support given to the other men.

Rob

Rob's behaviour with women staff was causing considerable concern. There were one or two whom he would not leave alone and if he did not get the attention he was seeking he would sometimes swear at them, using sexually explicit language. At a case conference, with Rob and his mother present, one woman who had been on the receiving end of this behaviour raised it for discussion. The chair of the meeting acknowledged that it was a problem but said it was too private to deal with in the meeting, and suggested that the two of them talked together afterwards.

Jeremy

Jeremy had been living in an institution for 20 years. He had been admitted initially because of a sexual assault against a child. Now that the hospital was closing, he was due to be resettled for the community. The resettlement team could not find any details of what the original sexual assault had been.

Richard

Richard had been referred for sexual counselling after he had grabbed the breast of a woman at the day centre. During this work he said that he wanted to 'rape' this same woman. The counsellor did not report this statement to anyone in the service concerned but did discuss it with his external supervisor whose opinion was that 'it was good that Richard could express his aggression in the sessions'.

■ Do you think knowledge about these men's sexual behaviour had been appropriately recorded and passed on in these examples?

activity
3c Sharing information

One particular dilemma is whether people with learning disabilities should be directly warned of the risks of abusive sexual behaviour. Refer to the scenarios in **Activity 3.1: Service responsibility** to consider the following:

- Should women at the evening social club attended by Gregory have been told that if he said anything rude they could come and find a member of staff immediately?

- Should the women with whom Noah has struck up a relationship be offered any additional support?

- Should service-users at the day service Malcolm is referred to be given any advanced notice that their new colleague might be difficult?

activity

3d | Sharing information – 'Need to Know'

Victor

Victor has lived in a large group home for a number of years. On at least three occasions during this time he has been found forcing himself sexually on less able people – both women and men. It was clear that in no way was this contact invited. Recently he has started a relationship with a woman who lives at another group home but whom he sees at the day service. On a couple of occasions he has invited her to his house in the evening. When this took place staff were very careful not to leave them alone because they were afraid he might take advantage of her despite the relationship appearing mutual. Now he has been invited to her house and his staff are worried about what supervision will be available there and whether they should say anything.

■ Would you inform the staff in the woman's group home about Victor's history of abuse?

■ Would you want the woman herself to be informed about his history?

■ Would you want the woman's parents to be briefed about the developing relationship including giving them information about his history?

activity

3e | Assessing your local services

This list is designed to assess the ability of your local services to respond to men with learning disabilities who have unacceptable or abusive sexual behaviour. The more questions you are able to tick, the greater the possibility of a coherent response.

Is there joint commissioning between health and social services?	☐
Is case management by social services in place and effective at co-ordinating the service of an individual with learning disabilities?	☐
Do social services provide specialist case managers for people with learning disabilities?	☐
Do health and social services have a good understanding of the extent of local need?	☐
Do good relationships exist between key people responsible for learning disability services?	☐
Do forums exist which bring different services together to share experiences and to plan future initiatives?	☐

activity

3f | Finding the balance

Andrew

Andrew had committed a number of incidents of exposure to local children around the group home where he lived. The parents on each occasion did not want charges to be made. The staff tried to minimise the risk by operating a high level of informal supervision and requesting that he did not go out without staff. Unfortunately, Andrew was not compliant with this regime and he managed to commit a further offence. The staff recognised that they could not guarantee an adequate level of safety for the children in the locality, and reluctantly agreed that he should move to an isolated institution where it would be easier to control the risk to children. They openly acknowledged that this was not in Andrew's best interests, because his personal development, which they had worked hard to support, would suffer greatly within the institution.

William

William's history of sexual assaults against less able people in the institution where he used to live had resulted in him being prescribed medication which was intended to be a sexual suppressant. He remained on this drug after he moved to the community. Staff there were concerned about the side effects, in particular how his breasts had developed, and raised the subject with his GP who said it would be at their risk if the medication was withdrawn. Staff were also worried it might effect any sexual contact he might have with his current girlfriend who was unaware of his abusive past.

Graham

A woman with learning disabilities whose breast had been grabbed at the day centre by Graham was very upset by the incident. Her key worker at the residential unit argued that it was not right that she should be expected to continue going to the day service with him, and tried to persuade the centre to exclude Graham indefinitely. This was unsuccessful and all that was achieved was a verbal commitment that he would be watched more carefully.

---

continued...

activity

3f   Finding the balance (continued)

Siad

Siad had caused considerable problems because of his staring at women and children when he went out alone to the local shops. The most recent incident involved him following two young boys into the park. There had been no sexual contact but the boys had been worried enough about the incident to tell their parents who demanded that Siad was not to be allowed out by himself again. Although there had not been one recorded incident of indecent assault in Siad's past, staff were very worried about how the local community might react if they saw him out alone, particularly since there had already been a lot of resistance to the group home. As a consequence they instructed Siad to stay in unless there was a staff member who could escort him. Siad was not happy about this but was compliant with the instruction.

■ What ethical dilemmas were faced in each of the above situations?

■ What decisions would you have made and why?

Case checklists

case checklist

A Starting off

Before you start: who is the right person to co-ordinate this process of assessment, decision making and care planning? Is it you? Do you have a mandate to intervene?

If you think a man has unacceptable or abusive sexual behaviour:

☐ Has the immediate risk of abuse continuing against the same person or others been addressed?

No – protect vulnerable people by separation and supervision.

☐ Is there a policy which covers this issue in your organisation?

Yes – follow policy.

No – inform your manager of the situation so they can take responsibility.

☐ **Should the police be involved?**

Yes – involve at the earliest possible opportunity. Do not undertake any further inquiries yourself without first consulting the investigating officers.

No – record the reasons why they were not involved for future reference. Remember the service may need to justify this to advocates or purchasing authorities.

☐ **Have the people who indicated and/or were first alerted to the possibility that abuse may have taken place made written records of what happened?**

Yes – Ensure they are signed, dated and held securely by a responsible manager.

No – These to be completed immediately. In the case of people who have limited written skills, they may want to dictate or record on tape.

case checklist

B Collecting information

To draw up an accurate picture of the man's sexual behaviour:

Talk to the following people:

☐ the man himself

☐ the victim

☐ potential victims to include vulnerable people the man meets at home or in learning disability services

☐ witnesses or those first alerted

☐ people who have known the man well over a period of time to provide a historical perspective on his behaviour – these may include direct care staff and/or parents and carers

☐ people in other settings – they may have a different understanding of the same behaviour. This could include professionals such as psychiatrists, speech or other therapists who have had contact with the man.

Check the following records:

☐ the man's current case file

☐ the service's day book

☐ records from other services the man has contact with

☐ records from specialists with whom the man has had contact, for example psychologists

☐ records from services with which the man has had previous contact

☐ central files held by the purchasing authority.

Record any contradictions, particularly if you are still not certain what in fact took place.

case checklist

$\boxed{\text{C}}$ Recording the behaviour

☐ What is believed to have happened?

☐ What sexual acts/behaviour were involved?

☐ Who was the victim and what is their relationship to the man? (For example, women staff member, less able person with learning disabilities, girlfriend)

☐ How was the above information established? (For example, talking to the victim, witnessed)

☐ What response to the man has been made to date? (For example, reprimanded verbally, suspended from day service)

☐ What other responses have been made? (For example, support for victim, contacted the police)

☐ Effect of response to the man's attitudes and behaviour

case checklist

D Networks

Use this table to depict the network of the man whose behaviour you are concerned about.

Family	Peers	Friends	Paid carers

case checklist

E | Identifying factors

In trying to understand the possible origins of the man's behaviour, explore all the sources of information identified in **Case Checklist B: Collecting information**. *Use this to identify factors under the following headings:*

- Physical appearance

- Medical conditions

- Mental health issues

- Drugs – prescribed and others (including alcohol)

- Knowledge about sex including remembering responses to earlier incidents

- Sexual interests

- Messages in his environment about what are appropriate and inappropriate behaviours and sexual attitudes

- Limited attachments and social networks

- Self-esteem.

case checklist

F Finkelhor's model

Use **Finkelhor's Model** to draw up your own picture of why your man is sexually abusing:

FINKELHOR'S MODEL		
Motivation to abuse	*Overcoming internal inhibitors*	*Overcoming external inhibitors*	*Overcoming the resistance of victims*

Highlight the issues above which particularly contribute to current risk in relation to his sexual behaviour.

*Keep this checklist with you as you read about possible responses to the man's behaviour in **Part Three**.*

case checklist

G Degree of responsibility

Think about the man you are concerned about. Where on a continuum between **'Couldn't help it'** and **'In control'** would you judge this man to be? Put a cross on the line below or, if you are reviewing this case in a group draw one up on a flip chart and ask everyone to put up a cross and then review the different positions you have all taken.

Couldn't help it ◄—————————————————► **In control**

Identify the different reasons for the judgement and list them under the following two headings:

Reasons why the man may not be fully responsible for his behaviour:

Reasons why the man should be held responsible for his behaviour:

If you do this in a group or staff meeting you will want to discuss the validity of some of the reasons given.

case checklist

H | Informing other services of risks

This information should be provided to any service and agency where the man's behaviour poses a risk to people there:

- **What sexual risk does the man pose to other people?** (For example, exposing himself, touching through clothing without consent, verbal harassment.)

- **Who is vulnerable?** (For example, other people with learning disabilities, women staff, specific [named] individuals.)

- **Which services and individuals need to be informed of the risk?** (For example, work support, social clubs, family members.)

- **What strategies are advised to minimise the risk in each service?**

- **Has each service produced a strategy for preventing the man from abusing and responding to any actual incidents of abuse?**

- **Are there any services which the man should not access because of the unacceptable degree of risk?**

- **When was the risk last reviewed?** It is important that a record is made of this so that services are not being alerted to a risk which has long since gone, or are unwarned about increased risk.

Note: Use *Case checklist I: Sexual risk disclosure sheet* as a pro forma for passing on information to individuals and services about the sexual risks the man poses.

case checklist

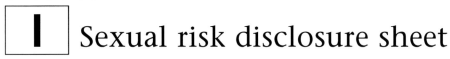

1 | Sexual risk disclosure sheet

Below is information about a service-user who poses a sexual risk to others. This information is provided so that preventive strategies can be put in place to protect people from abuse and also to protect the man's placement in the service.

Client's name

Current residence

Nature of the sexual risk

Who is vulnerable? *(name individuals where appropriate)*

How frequently does this occur? *(if infrequent, give date on which abuse last occurred)*

What strategies are advised to minimise the risk of abuse?

Required response to similar incidents of abuse *(for example, inform police, notify purchasing authority)*

Form written and sent by

Name	Position

Service	

Signature	Date

Form received by

Name	Position

Service	

Signature	Date

This form to be copied and kept on file in both organisations for future reference.

case checklist

$\boxed{J}$ Care planning

Care plans should address the following three areas:

1 Immediate responses

Consider:

- police involvement
- sanctions
- suspension
- supervision.

2 Sex education

Ensure he understands:

- what he has done is wrong
- this is the reason for the consequences
- the potential consequences of further abuse.

3 Long-term planning

Consider:

- change of service
- enriching his life
- counselling/therapy.

case checklist

K | Ethics

■ What rights are at stake? For example, freedom of movement, confidentiality.

■ In what way is the intervention in the man's interest? For example, to maintain his residence in the community?

■ What are the interests of the victims/potential victims? Who is representing these?

■ Are the responses comparable to those which other men would receive? How can any discrepancy be justified?

■ What are the resource implications, for the man himself and the service generally?

■ What does the man with learning disabilities think about the proposed responses to his behaviour?

■ Has formal authority for decision making been sought?

References

ADSS/NAPSAC (1996) *Advice for Social Services Departments on Abuse of People with Learning Disabilities in Residential Care*. Northallerton & Nottingham: ADSS/NAPSAC.

Atkinson D & Williams P (1990) *Mental Handicap: Changing Perspectives Workbook 2 – Networks*. Milton Keynes: Open University.

BBC 2 (13 November 1991) *Public Eye: A Betrayal of Trust*. London: BBC.

Bear D, Freeman R & Greenberg M (1984) Behavioural Alterations in Patients with Temporal Lobe Epilepsy. In: B Brummer (Ed) *Psychiatric Aspects of Epilepsy*. Washington: American Psychiatric Press.

Boeringer S (1996) Influences of fraternity membership athletics and male living arrangements on sexual aggression. *Violence against Women* **2** (2) 134–147.

British Association for Counselling (1990) *Code of Ethics and Practice for Counsellors*. Rugby: BAC.

Brown H (1989) Whose 'Ordinary Life' is it anyway? *Disability Handicap & Society* **4** (2) 105–119.

Brown H (1996) *Towards Safer Commissioning: A handbook for purchasers and commissioners on the sexual abuse of adults with learning disabilities*. Part of the Need to Know Series. Nottingham: NAPSAC. Distributed by Pavilion Publishing (Brighton).

Brown H (1998) *A Fine Line (Unit 22): Understanding Health and Social Welfare Course Workbook*. Milton Keynes: Open University.

Brown H, Brammer A, Craft A & McKay C (1996) *Towards Better Safeguards: A handbook for inspectors and registration officers on the sexual abuse of adults with learning disabilities*. Part of the Need to Know Series. Nottingham: NAPSAC. Distributed by Pavilion Publishing (Brighton).

Brown H & Cambridge P (1995) Contracting for Change: Making contracts work for people with learning disabilities. In: T Philpot & L Ward (Eds) *Values and Visions: Changing Ideas in Services for People with Learning Disabilities* pp50–80. Oxford: Butterworth Heinemann.

Brown H & Craft A (1989) *Thinking the unthinkable: papers on sexual abuse and people with mental handicap (Report of the first national conference on sexual abuse of people with learning disabilities)*. London: FPA.

Brown H & Egan-Sage E with Barry G & McKay C (1996) *Towards Better Interviewing: A handbook for police officers and social workers on the sexual abuse of adults with learning disabilities.* Part of the Need to Know Series. Nottingham: NAPSAC. Distributed by Pavilion Publishing (Brighton).

Brown H, Stein J & Turk V (1995) The sexual abuse of adults with learning disabilities: report of a second two year incidence survey. *Mental Handicap Research* **9** (1) 3–24.

Brown H & Stein J (1997) Sexual abuse perpetrated by men with learning disabilities: a comparative study. *Journal of Intellectual Disabilities Research* **41** (3) 215–224.

Brown H & Thompson D (1997a) The ethics of research with men who have learning disabilities and abusive sexual behaviour: a minefield in a vacuum. *Disability and Society* **12** (5) 695–707.

Brown H & Thompson D (1997b) Service responses to men with learning disabilities who have sexually abusive or unacceptable behaviours: the case against inaction. *Journal of Applied Research in Intellectual Disability* **10** (2) 176–197.

Brown H & Thompson D (1997c) Men with intellectual disabilities who sexually abuse: a review of the literature. *Journal of Applied Research in Intellectual Disability* **10** (2) 140–158.

Brown H & Turk V (1992) Defining sexual abuse as it affects adults with learning disabilities. *Mental Handicap* **20** (2) 44–55.

Cambridge P (1997) How far to Gay? The politics of HIV in learning disability. *Disability and Society* **12** (3) 427–453.

Charman T & Clare I (1992) Education about the laws and social rules relating to sexual behaviour. *Mental Handicap* **20** (2) 44–55.

Churchill J, Brown H, Craft A & Horrocks C (Eds) (1997) *There Are No Easy Answers: Service needs of people with learning disabilities who sexually abuse others.* Chesterfield/Nottingham: ARC/NAPSAC.

Clare ICH (1993) Issues in the assessment and treatment of male sexual offenders with mild learning disabilities. *Sexual and Marital Therapy* **8** (2) 167–180.

Clare ICH & Carson D (1997) Boundaries with the Criminal Justice System and Other Legal Systems. In: J Churchill *et al* (Eds) *There Are No Easy Answers: Service needs of people with learning disabilities who sexually abuse others.* Chesterfield/ Nottingham: ARC/NAPSAC.

Cooper AJ (1995) Review of the role of antilibidinal drugs in the treatment of sex offenders with mental retardation. *Mental Retardation* **33** 42–48.

Corbet A (1996) *Trinity of Pain.* London: RESPOND.

Craft A (1986) Sexual social and emotional development in people with Down's Syndrome. *Mental Handicap* **14** 33–36.

Craft A (Ed) (1994) *Practice Issues in Sexuality and Learning Disabilities.* London: Routledge.

Crossmaker M (1991) Behind locked doors – Institutional sexual abuse. *Sexuality and Disability* **9** (3) 201–219.

Day K (1994) Male mentally handicapped sex offenders. *British Journal of Psychiatry* **165** 630–639.

Department of Health (1996) *Building Bridges: A guide to the arrangements for interagency working for the care and protection of severely mentally ill people.* London: HMSO.

Department of Health (2000) *No Secrets: Guidance on developing and implementing multi-agency policies and procedures to protect vulnerable adults from abuse.* London: DH.

Department of Health (2001) *Valuing People.* London: DH.

Department of Health (2003) *Care Homes for Adults* (18–65). London: DH.

Dworkin A (1981) *Pornography: Men Possessing Women.* London: The Women's Press.

Faban J & Wexler S (1988) Explanations of sexual assault among violent delinquents. *Journal of Adolescent Research* **3** 363–385.

Fairbairn G, Rowley D & Bowen M (1995) *Sexuality, Learning Difficulties and Doing What's Right.* London: David Fulton Publishers.

Finkelhor D (1986) *A Source Book on Child Sexual Abuse.* London: Sage.

Finkelhor D (Ed) (1984) *Child Sexual Abuse: New Theory and Research.* New York: Free Press.

Flynn M, Whelan E & Speake B (1985) The mentally handicapped adult's concepts of good and bad acts. *Journal of Mental Deficiency Research* **29** 55–62.

Flynn M & Brown H (1997) Commissioning Safer Services. In: J Churchill *et al* (Eds) *There Are No Easy Answers: Service needs of people with learning disabilities who sexually abuse others* pp36–52. Chesterfield/Nottingham: ARC/NAPSAC.

Gebherd PM (1973) Sexual Behaviour of the Mentally Retarded. In: F De la Cruz & G Laveck (Eds) *Human Sexuality and the Mentally Retarded.* London: Butterworths.

Gilby R, Wolf L & Golberg B (1989) Mentally retarded adolescent sex offenders: a survey and pilot study. *Canadian Journal of Psychiatry* **34** (6) 542–8.

Haaven J (1983) Taped site interview by FH Knopp 17 October. In: FH Knopp (1984) *Retraining Adult Sex Offenders: Methods and Models*. Synacuise: Safer Society Press.

Hames A (1987) Sexual offences involving children: a suggested treatment for adolescents with mild mental handicap. *Mental Handicap* **15** 19–21.

Hayes S (1991) Sex offenders. *Australian and New Zealand Journal of Development Disabilities* **172** 221–227.

Heyman B & Huckle S (1995) Sexuality as a perceived hazard in the lives of adults with learning difficulties. *Disability and Society* **10** (2) 139–157.

Hingsburger D (1987) Sex counselling with the developmentally handicapped: the assessment and management of seven critical problems. *Psychiatric Aspects of Mental Retardation Reviews* **6** (9) 41–46.

Hingsburger D, Griffiths D & Quinsey V (1991) Detected counterfeit deviance: differentiating sexual deviance from sexual inappropriateness. *The Habilitative Mental Health Newsletter* **10** (9) 51–54.

Hogwood B & Gunn L (1984) *Policy Analysis for the Real World*. Milton Keynes: Open University Press.

Horizon NHS Trust (1997) *Report of the Independent Panel of Inquiry*. Horizon NHS Trust.

Hummel P, Aschoff W, Blessman F & Anders O (1993) Sexually aggressive acts of an adolescent with Klinefelter Syndrome. *Uprax-Kinderpsychologie-Kinderpsychiatrie* **42** (4) 132–138.

Kelly L, Wingfield R, Burton S & Regan L (1995) *Splintered Lives: Sexual exploitation of children in the context of children's rights and child protection*. Ilford: Barnardos.

Lachmann M, Brzek A, Mellan J, Hampl R, Starka L & Motlik K (1991) Recidivous offence in sadistic homosexual paedophiles with Karyotype 48 XXXY after testicular pulpectomy. *Experimental Clinical Endocrinology* **98** (2) 171–174.

Laurance BM (1993) Prader-Willi Syndrome. *Pediatric Review Community* **7** 77–91.

Linsay WR (2002) Research and literature on sex offenders with intellectual and developmental disabilities. *Journal of Intellectual Disabilities* **46** (supplement 1) 74–85.

Lisman WA (1987) *Organic Psychiatry*. Oxford: Blackwells.

Marshall W (1993) The role of attachments intimacy and loneliness in the aetiology and maintenance of sexual offending. *Sexual and Marital Therapy* **8** (2) 109–121.

Marshall W, Laws D & Barbaree H (1990) *Handbook of Sexual Assault*. London: Plenum Press.

McCarthy M (1993) Sexual experiences of women with learning difficulties in long-stay hospitals. *Sexuality and Disability* **11** (4) 277–285.

McCarthy M & Thompson D (1993) *Sex and Staff Training*. Brighton: Pavilion Publishing.

McCarthy M & Thompson D (1996) Sexual abuse by design: an examination of the issues in learning disability services. *Disability and Society* **11** (2) 205–217.

McCarthy M & Thompson D (1997) A prevalence study of sexual abuse of adults with intellectual disabilities referred for sex education. *Journal of Applied Research In Intellectual Disability* **10** (2) 105–124.

McCarthy M & Thompson D (1998) *Sex and the 3Rs*. Brighton: Pavilion Publishing.

McCarthy M & Thompson D (2004) People with Learning Disabilities: Sex the Law and Consent. In: M Cowling and P Reynolds (Eds) *Making Sense of Sexual Consent*. Aldershot: Ashgate.

Mencap & The Law Society (1995) *Mentally Vulnerable Witnesses in Criminal Proceedings: A report of a joint seminar*. London: Mencap.

Murphy G & Clare ICH (1991) MIETS II Assessment treatment outcome for service-users and service effectiveness. *Mental Handicap Research* **4** 180–206.

Murrey GH, Briggs D & Davis C (1992) Psychopathically disordered mentally ill and mentally handicapped sex offenders: a comparative study. *Medicine Science and the Law* **32** (4) 331–336.

O'Connor W (1994) *A Preliminary Report on Intervention with Sex Offenders with an Intellectual Disability*. Melbourne Australia: Centre for Social Health.

Pyeritz RE & McKusick VA (1979) The Marfan Syndrome: diagnosis and management. *New England Journal of Medicine* **71** 784–790.

Raboch J, Mellan K & Starka L (1979) Klinefelter's Syndrome: Sexual development and activity. *Archives of Sexual Behaviour* **8** (4) 333–9.

Raboch J, Cernal H & Zemek P (1987) Sexual aggressitivity and androgens. *British Journal of Psychiatry* **151** 398–400.

Sgroi SM (1989) *Vulnerable Populations*. Toronto: Lexington Books.

Sheridan R, Lierena J, Natkins S & Debenham P (1989) Fertility in a male with trisomy 21. *Journal of Medical Genetics* **26** 294–298.

Sinason V (1992) *Mental Handicap and the Human Condition*. London: Free Association Books or contact RESPOND London and Tavistock Clinic.

Sobsey R (1994) *Violence and Abuse in the Lives of People with Disabilities*. Baltimore: Paul H Brookes.

Sorensen K (1992) Physical and mental development of adolescent males with Klinefelter's Syndrome. *Hormone Research* **37** (3) 55–61.

Stein J & Brown H (1995) All in this together: an evaluation of joint training on the abuse of adults with learning disabilities. *Health and Social Care in the Community* **3** (4) 205–214.

Sullivan G & Lukoff D (1990) Sexual side effects of antipsychotic medications: evaluation and interventions. *Hospital and Community Psychiatry* **41** (1) 1238–1241.

Swanson CK & Garwick GB (1990) Treatment for low functioning sex offenders: Group therapy and interagency co-ordination. *Mental Retardation* **28** (3) 155–161.

Thompson D (1994a) The sexual experiences of men with learning disabilities who have sex with men: Issues for HIV prevention. *Sexuality and Disability* **12** 221–242.

Thompson D (1994b) Sexual experience and sexual identity for men with learning disabilities who have sex with men. *Changes* **12** (4) 254–263.

Thompson D (1997a) A Review of the Literature. In: J Churchill *et al* (Eds) *There Are No Easy Answers: Service needs of people with learning disabilities who sexually abuse others.* Chesterfield/Nottingham: ARC/NAPSAC.

Thompson D (1997b) Profiling the sexually abusive behaviour of men with intellectual disabilities. *Journal of Applied Research in Intellectual Disability* **10** (2) 125–139.

Thompson D, Clare I & Brown H (1997) Not such an 'ordinary' relationship: the role of women support staff in relation to men with learning disabilities who have difficult sexual behaviour. *Disability and Society* **12** (4) 573–592.

Verberne G (1990) Treatment of sexually deviant behaviours in mildly mentally retarded adults. In: A Dosen, A Van Gennep & GJ Zwanikkeen (Eds) *Treatment of Mental Illness and Behavioural Disorders in the Mentally Retarded* pp374–386. Leiden, The Netherlands: Logal Publications.

Waterhouse L, Dobash RP & Carnie J (1994) *Child Sexual Abusers.* Edinburgh: Central Research Unit, The Scottish Office.

Watkins B & Bentovin A (1992) The sexual abuse of male children and adolescents: a review of current research. *Journal of Child Psychology* **33** 197–248.

Watney S (1989) *Policing Desire – Pornography AIDS and the Media.* University of Minnesota Press.

Wilson JD & Foster DW (Eds) (1985) *Williams Textbook of Endocrinology.* Toronto: WB Saunders Co.

Wyre R (1990) *Women, Men and Rape.* London: Perry Publications.

Related publications

The research led directly and indirectly to the publication of a number of papers in books and academic journals which may provide useful supplementary reading:

Brown H & Stein J (1997) Sexual abuse perpetrated by men with learning disabilities: a comparative study. *Journal of Intellectual Disabilities Research* **41** (3) 215–224.

Brown H & Thompson D (1997a) The ethics of research with men who have learning disabilities and abusive sexual behaviour: a minefield in a vacuum. *Disability and Society* **12** (5) 695–707.

Brown H & Thompson D (1997b) Service responses to men with learning disabilities who have sexually abusive or unacceptable behaviours: the case against inaction. *Journal of Applied Research in Intellectual Disability* **10** (2) 176–197.

Brown H & Thompson D (1997c) Men with intellectual disabilities who sexually abuse: a review of the literature. *Journal of Applied Research in Intellectual Disability* **10** (2) 140–158.

Churchill J, Brown H, Craft A & Horrocks C (Eds) (1997) *There Are No Easy Answers: Service needs of people with learning disabilities who sexually abuse others.* Chesterfield/Nottingham: ARC/NAPSAC.

Flynn M & Brown H (1997) Commissioning Safer Services. In: J Churchill, H Brown, A Craft & C Horrocks (Eds) (1997) *There Are No Easy Answers* pp36–52. Chesterfield/Nottingham: ARC/NAPSAC.

Thompson D (1997a) A Review of the Literature. In: J Churchill, H Brown, A Craft & C Horrocks (Eds) (1997) *There Are No Easy Answers* pp36–52. Chesterfield/Nottingham: ARC/NAPSAC.

Thompson D (1997b) Profiling the sexually abusive behaviour of men with intellectual disabilities. *Journal of Applied Research in Intellectual Disability* **10** (2) 125–139.

Thompson D (2001) Is sex a good thing for men with learning disabilities? *Tizard Learning Disability Review* **6** (1) 4–12.

Thompson D, Clare I & Brown H (1997) Not such an 'ordinary' relationship: the role of women support staff in relation to men with learning disabilities who have difficult sexual behaviour. *Disability and Society* **12** (4) 573–592.

Further reading

Since publication of the first edition a number of studies have been carried out and further work undertaken. Readers might find the following references helpful.

Ashman L & Duggan L (2004) Interventions for Learning-Disabled Sex Offenders (Cochrane Review). In: *The Cochrane Library* Issue 4 2004. Chichester UK: John Wiley & Sons Ltd.

Boswell G & Wedge P (2003) A pilot evaluation of a therapeutic community for adolescent male sexual abusers. *Therapeutic Communities* **24** (4) 259–276.

Broxholme SL & Lindsay WR (2003) Development and preliminary evaluation of a questionnaire on cognitions related to sex offending for use with individuals who have mild intellectual disabilities. *Journal of Intellectual Disability Research* **47** (6) 472–482.

Cambridge P & Mellan B (2000) Reconstructing the sexuality of men with learning disabilities: empirical evidence and theoretical interpretations of need. *Disability & Society* **15** (2) 293–311.

Courtney J & Rose J (2004) The effectiveness of treatment for male sex offenders with learning disabilities: a review of the literature. *Journal of Sexual Aggression* **10** (2) 215–236.

El-Leity S (1998) Assessing sexual interest in clients with learning disabilities using a card-sort task. *Sexual and Marital Therapy* **13** (1) 51–62.

Fyson R, Eadie T & Cooke P (2003) Adolescents with learning disabilities who show sexually inappropriate or abusive behaviors: development of a research study. *Child Abuse Review* **12** (5) 305–314.

Green G, Gray NS & Willner P (2003) Management of sexually inappropriate behaviors in men with learning disabilities. *The Journal of Forensic Psychiatry & Psychology* **14** (1) 85–110.

Jahoda A (2002) Offenders with a learning disability: the evidence for better services? *Journal of Applied Research in Intellectual Disabilities* **15** (2) 175–178.

Lindsay WR, Smith AHW, Law J, Quinn K, Anderson A, Smith A & Allan R (2004) Sexual and nonsexual offenders with intellectual and learning disabilities: a comparison of characteristics referral patterns and outcomes. *Journal of Interpersonal Violence* **19** (8) 875–890.

O'Callaghan D (1998) Practice issues in working with young abusers who have learning disabilities. *Child Abuse Review* **7** (6) 435–448.

Parry CJ & Lindsay WR (2003) Impulsiveness as a factor in sexual offending by people with mild intellectual disability. *Journal of Intellectual Disability Research* **47** (6) 483–487.

Sequeira H & Hollins S (2003) Clinical effects of sexual abuse on people with learning disability: critical literature review. *British Journal of Psychiatry* **181** 13–19.

Thompson D (2000) Vulnerability dangerousness and risk: the case of men with learning disabilities who sexually abuse. *Health Risk & Society* **2** (1) 33–46.

Walsh A (2000) Improve and care: responding to inappropriate masturbation in people with severe intellectual disabilities. *Sexuality and Disability* **18** (1) 27–39.

Useful organisations

Consent (formerly the Sex Education Team)
Administration Building
Woodside Road
Abbots Langley
Herts WD5 0HT
Telephone: 01923 670796
www.hertsparts.nhs.uk/consent

> **Consent** offer direct work with people with learning disabilities on a range of sexual issues including working with men who sexually abuse. They can provide consultancy and training to staff.

**The Foundation for People with Learning Disabilities &
The Mental Health Foundation**
Sea Containers House
20 Upper Ground
London SE1 9QB
Telephone: 020 7803 1100
www.mentalhealth.org.uk
www.learningdisabilities.org.uk

> The Foundation for People with Learning Disabilities is part of the Mental Health Foundation. They provide information and fund research on learning disability and mental health.

The Ann Craft Trust (ACT)
Centre for Social Work
University of Nottingham
University Park
Nottingham NG7 2RD
Telephone: 0115 951 5400
www.anncrafttrust.org

> The Ann Craft Trust (formerly NAPSAC) works with staff in the statutory, independent and voluntary sectors in the interest of people with learning disabilities who may be at risk from abuse.

NOTA – The National Association for the Treatment of Abusers
PO Box 356
Hull HU12 8WR
www.nota.co.uk

> NOTA have local networks for people working with sex offenders. They also organise conferences and training.

RESPOND
Third Floor
24–32 Stephenson Way
London NW1 2HD
Telephone: 020 7383 0700 / 0808 808 0700
www.respond.org.uk

> RESPOND can provide psychotherapy for people with learning disabilities who are either the victims or perpetrators of sexual abuse. They also offer consultancy and training.

SALOMONS
Practice Consultancy Unit
Salomons
Canterbury Christ Church University College
Broomhill Road
Southborough
Tunbridge Wells
Kent TN4 8NS
Telephone: 01892 515152
Practice.consultancy@salomons.org.uk
www.salomons.org.uk

The Practice Consultancy Unit within the Centre for Applied Social and Psychological Development provides a range of consultancy, research and mentoring around social care issues including abuse of vulnerable adults, capacity and consent, sexuality and disability and palliative care issues in relation to people with learning disabilities: contact Professor Hilary Brown.

The Tizard Centre
Beverly Farm
University of Kent at Canterbury
Canterbury
Kent CT2 7LZ
Telephone: 01227 764000
www.kent.ac.uk/tizard/

The **Tizard Centre** provides courses and consultancy in the areas of learning disability and mental health. They have a wide experience of work on sexual issues for people with learning disabilities.

VOICE UK
Wyvern House
Railway Terrace
Derby DE1 2RU
Telephone: 01332 295775
www.voiceuk.org.uk

VOICE UK is a voluntary organisation which exists to support people with learning disabilities and their families around issues of abuse and abusing. It conducts research, provides advice and advocates for individuals who are taking cases through the criminal justice system.

Young Abusers Project
Peckwater Resource Centre
6 Peckwater Street
London NW5 2TX
Telephone: 020 7530 6422

Managed by the NSPCC, the **Young Abusers Project** provides assessment and treatment for people aged 6–21 where there is concern about sexually abusive behaviour to others; they have experience of working with young men with learning disabilities.

Also available from Pavilion

Living Safer Sexual Lives

A training and resource pack for people with learning disabilities and those who support them

Patsie Frawley, Kelley Johnson, Lynne Hillier and Lyn Harrison

This internationally piloted resource provides training on sexuality and sexual rights for everyone involved in the lives of people with learning disabilities, including the individuals themselves. This easily accessible training pack supports learning about values, attitudes, safety and rights in relation to sexuality and relationships for people with learning disabilities, their families and friends, service providers and staff.

The pack includes a video featuring three actors with learning disabilities relating three of the stories included in the pack.

Format: ringbound resource (260pp) and video (27 mins)

ISBN: 1 84196 115 9

Keeping Safe

A modular teaching resource to develop skills for people with learning disabilities to minimise risk of abuse

Home Farm Trust

This modular resource aims to help people with learning disabilities to develop an awareness of their rights, abilities and strengths, and provides the opportunity to develop skills to counter abuse, with a particular focus on sexual abuse. It also gives them information about their rights and responsibilities within consensual relationships, and can be adapted to individual circumstances.

Format: 3 ringbinders (100pp/328pp/69pp), facilitator's guidebook, participant's handbook and illustrated line drawings resource.

Thumbs Up!

Assertiveness skills for people who have learning disabilities

Deanne Bell

Assertiveness skills training is increasingly recognised to be a valuable part of personal development. The *Thumbs Up!* training resource emphasises a holistic approach to personal development, and highlights the link between self-esteem and behaviour. This resource presents information for the facilitator in a flexible format and includes activities, key points and aims for each session.

Participants are encouraged to develop and practice assertiveness skills, recognise the importance of the effect of self-esteem on behaviour and develop strategies for raising self-esteem.

Format: ringbound materials including illustrations, handouts and worksheets (84pp)

ISBN: 1 900600 59 5

Positive Goals

Interventions for people with learning disabilities whose behaviour challenges

Peter Ferns and Eric Emerson

Written by eminent professionals in the field, *Positive Goals* is a resource pack which aims to help carers and professionals to identify meaningful, appropriate and socially valid interventions for people with learning disabilities whose behaviour challenges. It also provides the means to evaluate the interventions by measuring outcomes against agreed goals.

The tool is consistent with the principals of person-centred planning and facilitates an inclusive approach by ensuring all relevant stakeholders have a say in the person's support or intervention plan.

Format: ringbound resource (70pp)

ISBN: 1 84196 105 1